COMBAT AIRCRAFT
159
HEINKEL He 219 UNITS

SERIES EDITOR TONY HOLMES

159 | COMBAT AIRCRAFT

Martin Streetly

HEINKEL He 219 UNITS

Osprey
PUBLISHING

OSPREY PUBLISHING
Bloomsbury Publishing Plc
Kemp House, Chawley Park, Cumnor Hill, Oxford, OX2 9PH, UK
Bloomsbury Publishing Ireland Limited,
29 Earlsfort Terrace, Dublin 2, D02 AY28, Ireland
1359 Broadway, 12th Floor, New York, NY 10018, USA
E-mail; info@ospreypublishing.com
www.ospreypublishing.com

OSPREY is a trademark of Osprey Publishing Ltd

First published in Great Britain in 2026

© Osprey Publishing Ltd, 2026

All rights reserved. No part of this publication may be: (i) reproduced or transmitted in any form or by any means, electronic or mechanical, including photocopying, recording, or any information storage or retrieval system, without prior permission in writing from the publishers; or (ii) used or reproduced in any way for the training, development, or operation of artificial intelligence (AI) technologies, including generative AI technologies. The rights holders expressly reserve this publication from the text and data mining exception as per Article 4(3) of the Digital Single Market Directive (EU) 2019 / 790.

A catalogue record for this book is available from the British Library.

ISBN: PB 9781472867919; eBook 9781472867926; ePDF 9781472867933; XML 9781472867902

26 27 28 29 30   10 9 8 7 6 5 4 3 2 1

Edited by Tony Holmes
Cover Artwork by Gareth Hector
Aircraft Profiles by Janusz Światłoń
Index by Alison Worthington
Typeset by Lumina Datamatics Ltd
Printed by Repro India Ltd

Osprey Publishing supports the Woodland Trust, the UK's leading woodland conservation charity.

To find out more about our authors and books visit www.ospreypublishing.com. Here you will find extracts, author interviews, details of forthcoming events and the option to sign up for our newsletter.

For product safety related questions contact productsafety@bloomsbury.com

Dedication
Sue, 1951–2019.

Acknowledgements
The author wishes to recognise the help given (in alphabetic order) by Eddie J Creek, Robert Forsyth and Chris Goss in the preparation and illustration of this book, together with thanks to cover artist Gareth Hector and profile artist Janusz Światłoń, who have added a great deal to this project. Additionally, no author tackling an account of the combat history of the He 219 can fail to acknowledge the pioneering research carried out by R Francis Ferguson and Roland Remp.

Front Cover
During May 1943, NJG 1 received He 219 V7 Wk-Nr 190007 G9+DB, V8 Wk-Nr 190008 G9+EB and V9 Wk-Nr 190009 G9+FB for operational evaluation. On the night of 11–12 June 1943, NJG 1's Major Werner Streib and his bordfunker, Unteroffizier Helmut Fischer, took off from Venlo in G9+FB as part of the defence against an RAF Bomber Command raid on Düsseldorf. At 0105 hrs, Streib encountered No 408 Sqn Halifax B II JB792 and shot it down. Twenty-three minutes later, he added a second Halifax B II (JB972, again from No 408 Sqn) to the night's tally, with a third Halifax B II (HR719 of No 158 Sqn) going down at 0155 hrs. Streib destroyed Lancaster B II DS647 of No 115 Sqn 21 minutes later, followed by a fourth unidentified Halifax B II at 0222 hrs.

Breaking off combat, Streib now headed home to Venlo, where he discovered that his aircraft's landing flaps were not functioning and, in the ensuing hard landing, his aircraft was written off. When the wreck came to a halt, its cockpit section had broken off completely from the rest of the fuselage and its back was broken. Surprisingly, Streib emerged from the crash virtually unscathed, while Fischer suffered arm and leg injuries that put him out of action for the next six weeks. In this way (and in just under two-and-a-half hours), the He 219 made its little short of spectacular combat debut (*Cover Artwork by Gareth Hector*)

Previous Pages
During May 1944, Venlo-based I./NJG 1 received He 219A-0 Wk-Nr 190188, which was subsequently used as a backdrop to this crew photograph of Hauptmann Paul Förster (to the right of the pair) and his bordfunker, Feldwebel Ernst Böhmer. Förster's first known nightfighter assignment was as a Hauptmann with 2./NJG 1 during late June 1943. Three months later, on 23 September, he was appointed 2./NJG 1's *Staffelkapitän*, a position which was followed by his becoming *Kommandeur* of I./NJG 1 during September 1944. Just weeks later, on 1 October, Förster was killed when his He 219 crashed while testing blind approach landing equipment at Münster-Handorf airfield. He was posthumously promoted to the rank of Major. During his nightfighting career, Förster was credited with five confirmed victories (*EN Archive*)

CONTENTS

CHAPTER ONE
TORTUOUS BEGINNINGS AND PRODUCTION   **6**

CHAPTER TWO
INTO COMBAT   **18**

CHAPTER THREE
A NEW YEAR   **25**

CHAPTER FOUR
ENDGAME   **60**

CHAPTER FIVE
ANATOMY   **80**

APPENDICES   **92**

COLOUR PLATES COMMENTARY   92
BIBLIOGRAPHY   95
INDEX   96

A heavily re-touched photograph that gives an excellent impression of the He 219 V1's original configuration. Points to note are the aircraft's bulged cockpit canopy, four-bladed propellers, ventral and dorsal fuselage 'steps', small fins and rudders and short rear sections to its engine nacelles (*EN Archive*)

CHAPTER ONE

TORTUOUS BEGINNINGS AND PRODUCTION

Development of Germany's only purpose-built nightfighter can be traced back to an April 1940 proposal from Heinkel for a high-speed reconnaissance aircraft that bore the in-house designation P.1055. As such, this proposal envisaged an 11.4-tonne aeroplane with a 42 m² wing area, a range of 400 km and a maximum speed of 750 km/h. Power was to be provided by an internally mounted, 3500 hp Daimler-Benz DB 613 coupled engine.

By October 1940, the P.1055 was being considered for the fast bomber and *Zerstörer* (heavy fighter) roles, as well as for reconnaissance. Here, the *Zerstörer* version was to have had a wing area of 37 m², a maximum speed of 720 km/h at an altitude of 9000 m, a range of 2000 km and an armament of two forward-firing 20 mm MG 151/20 cannon and single examples of the 7.92 mm MG 81Z and 13 mm MG 131Z machine guns for defence.

While development of the P.1055 continued, by November 1940 Heinkel saw 'little hope' for a *Zerstörer* variant. Inspection of a P.1055 mock-up took place late that same month, and with the type's configuration now being generally approved, it was added by the *Reichsluftfahrtministerium* (German Air Ministry – RLM) to its development planning process.

Generaloberst Erhard Milch, who replaced Generaloberst Ernst Udet as *Generalluftzeugmeister u. Chef des Planungamt d. Lw/RLM* after the latter's suicide, made continuous efforts to halt He 219 production in favour of a nightfighter based on either the Ju 88 or Ju 188 throughout the Heinkel's career (*Chris Goss Collection*)

During the next three months, work was undertaken to refine the various proposals, and by December 1940 the RLM considered the project to have reached a state of maturity such as to warrant the allocation of an official type designation. Thus, the He 219 was born. By late February 1941, the original P.1055 concept had been replaced by a 'new' He 219, the mock-up for which was inspected on 26 March 1941.

Development continued (with another mock-up of a three-seat iteration being examined on 20 June 1941), and by the end of June the RLM had dropped the idea of an internal engine installation in favour of a pair of wing-mounted powerplants.

On 11 July, Generaloberst Ernst Udet, the Luftwaffe's then *Generalluftzeugmeister u. Chef des Planungamt d. Lw./RLM* (Aircraft Master General and Chief of the RLM's Air Force Planning Office who was subsequently succeeded by Generaloberst Erhard Milch following his suicide on 17 November 1941), warned Professor Ernst Heinkel that the He 219 was 'in serious jeopardy'. Ongoing problems in finding a suitable engine for the type had led the RLM to question its future. After another mock-up inspection on 17 July, Udet enquired of Heinkel whether the He 219 would be suitable for nightfighting – a lifeline that Heinkel grasped with both hands.

In pursuit of a nightfighter He 219, Ernst Heinkel canvassed both the RLM and operational crews for information on nightfighting procedures and centred his thinking on an interceptor that could counter the RAF's latest heavy bombers (then the Avro Manchester, the Handley Page Halifax and the Short Stirling).

On 14 August 1941, Heinkel requested Udet's approval for the switch from internal to wing-mounted engines, with the latter instructing that He 219 development should now centre on nightfighter and high-altitude reconnaissance/day and night *Zerstörer* variants. By the end of the month, Heinkel had presented the RLM with a re-worked He 219 that would fulfil the nightfighter role, with the following October seeing the revised He 219 being powered by a pair of DB 603 engines, accommodating a crew of two, having a tricycle undercarriage, provision for ejector seats and airborne radar and boasting an armament of six forward-firing MG 151/20 cannon and an MG 131Z machine gun for rear defence.

At the beginning of January 1942, it was decided to issue an He 219 production contract and to begin construction of the V1 prototype. By the end of the next month, 80 per cent of the necessary production drawings had been completed and a mock-up of the proposed nightfighter had been inspected and deemed to be 'essentially correct'. The type's avionic fit now included a FuG 202 radar, the FuG 135 *Uhu* (eagle owl) data transmission system, two FuG 16 ZY radios and a FuG 10 P radio. Again, the aircraft was configured for 'Y' fighter guidance system functionality and was to be capable of receiving *Reichsjägerwelle* (Reichs fighter wave) control broadcasts. For its part, the RLM requested the possible use of the GM-1 power boost system to increase the aircraft's maximum speed, together with armour plating for its airframe, cockpit and engines.

During March 1942, a mock-up of the nightfighter cockpit was completed (the last He 219 mock-up to be produced) and Heinkel embarked on what proved to be a protracted struggle to obtain DB 603 engines from Daimler-Benz.

The He 219's engine problems were exacerbated by a series of four RAF Bomber Command raids on Rostock and its environs that took place between 24–27 April 1942. The last of the four inflicted heavy damage on Heinkel's Rostock plant (luckily, the He 219 V1 survived it) and, as a result, the company's design bureau

General der Flieger Josef Kammhuber was the architect behind the Luftwaffe's *Nachtjagdverband*, and he was also a staunch supporter of the He 219 as a nightfighter. During 1942, he requested that a *Gruppe* of 20–30 such aircraft should be available for operations by April 1943 (*Chris Goss Collection*)

was relocated to the 'safer' Heidfeld (subsequently known as Schwechat) airfield outside Vienna, in Austria.

For his part, *General der Flieger* Josef Kammhuber (the then *Kommandierender General* of the Luftwaffe's XII *Fliegerkorps*, which was effectively its nightfighter arm), a great supporter of the He 219, now requested that the formation of a 20- to 30-strong operational He 219 nightfighter *Gruppe* should begin no later than April 1943.

On 14 June 1942, a conference chaired by Milch determined that while the He 219 met 'most of [the RLM's] nightfighter requirements', there needed to be a detailed requirement for a Bf 110 nightfighter replacement drawn up before there could be certainty that the He 219 would meet such a requirement. This 'astonished' Kammhuber, as did the statement that 'even as a successor, [the He 219] would not be available until 1945'.

Despite vigorous protests from the Luftwaffe's Command Staff, the idea of a Ju 188-based nightfighter was also raised – comments that led to the construction of a Ju 188 mock-up equipped with FuG 202 radar. This was completed during early 1943, at which time Kammhuber bowed to the inevitable and requested new nightfighter proposals from Junkers (which became the Ju 88G and the Ju 388), Focke-Wulf (the Fw 187 and the Ta 154) and Messerschmitt (the Me 210).

Despite this hiccup, the end of June 1942 saw the RLM advise Heinkel that the He 219 was earmarked for large-scale production at the rate of 200 per month beginning in 1943, with a pre-production series of 20 aircraft to be available by April of that year. Again, the 'zero' series aircraft were to be built at Schwechat (not Rostock-Marienehe, in Germany, and Mielec, in Poland, as Ernst Heinkel wanted), with the site for series production to be determined later.

By the end of August 1942, the Fw 187 was no longer being considered as an He 219 competitor and Heinkel had handed finalised He 219 drawings to the RLM. At this point, the aircraft's forward-firing armament was specified as six MG 151/20 cannon, with power to be provided by a pair of 1726 hp (take-off and emergency rating) DB 603A engines.

On 1 September the RLM announced an He 219 production plan that comprised 12 prototypes (there were eventually 41 such aircraft built or proposed) and 173 He 219A-0 ('zero' series) machines that were to be delivered between March 1943 and September 1944. Further production of 117 aircraft was expected to be possible from January 1944, subject to the availability of the necessary materials. Series production was now potentially to take place at Budzyn and Mielec, in Poland.

In an attempt to resolve the lingering doubts concerning the He 219 as a nightfighter, Kammhuber, Generalmajor Vohwald and Generalingenieur Walter Hertel now compared the performance diagrams for the Do 217J, He 219 and Ju 88C nightfighters, together with those of the projected Ju 188 and Me 210 nightfighter variants – an exercise that (together with estimates of the various raw material requirements) showed a 'clear advantage for the Heinkel design'.

The He 219 V1 made its maiden flight on 6 November 1942, an event that prompted Ernst Heinkel to write to Milch informing him

A still from a film taken of the He 219 V1 on its maiden flight on 6 November 1942 (*EN archive*)

that the prototype had flown ten days earlier than promised, and that no major problems had arisen during the flight. Perhaps Heinkel spoke too soon, for three days later the He 219 V1 lost its nosewheel while landing. The aircraft was subsequently under repair until the end of the month.

For his part, Milch authorised a revised He 219 production plan, with aircraft now scheduled to reach operational units in early 1944. On 19 November 1942, the He 219 V1 was demonstrated to Kammhuber at Rostock-Marienehe, by which time the He 219 V2, V3 and V4 were in final assembly at Schwechat. On 2 December the He 219 V1 was back in the factory for a series of modifications that included lengthening its fuselage by 940 mm, increasing the thickness of its skinning by 30 per cent and eliminating the fuselage 'steps' which were to have accommodated remotely controlled dorsal and ventral defensive gun turrets.

On 10 January 1943, the He 219 V2 made its maiden flight, and by the 15th of the month the He 219 V1 had completed 46 flights (30 hrs 40 min flying time). By the end of January, the He 219 had been classified as a 'top priority' project, and it was now planned to increase output to 50 aircraft per month by December 1944 and to 100 aircraft per month during 1945, providing that the promised performance and handling characteristics were achieved. Operational testing was to be carried out by *Nachtjagdgeschwader* (NJG) 1's first *Gruppe*, I./NJG 1, led by nightfighter ace Major Werner Streib.

Following conversion, the He 219 V1 was back in the air during January–February 1943, and it 'soon demonstrated the desired handling characteristics'. Elsewhere, February 1943 saw the He 219 V2 receive the new streamlined and lengthened fuselage (which was to be fitted to

An in-flight view of the He 219 V1 that highlights its overall RLM 22 *schwarz* (black) camouflage, RLM 21 *weiß* (white) national markings and the RLM 77 *dunkelgrau* (dark grey) presentations of its *Stammkenzeichen* (master identity code) on the sides of its fuselage and beneath its wings (*EN Archive*)

all such aircraft from the He 219 V7 onwards) and the decision taken to fit all subsequent examples (prototypes and production aircraft alike) with enlarged fins and rudders to improve longitudinal stability. It was also decided to deliver the He 219 V7 and V8 to NJG 1 for service trials by mid-May 1943. Subsequently, the V9 aircraft was added to this roster too.

As was the case throughout its history, the He 219 programme suffered a sudden *volte-face* when, on 18 March 1943, the RLM requested cancellation of the aircraft so that Heinkel could concentrate on rectifying the He 177 heavy bomber's numerous faults. Despite this (and reflecting the increasingly Byzantine nature of the forward progress of the programme as a whole), Oberst Viktor von Loßberg, in his capacity as Commissar for the He 219 programme, ordered production to be decentralised, with fuselages to be built at Mielec/Budzyn and then flown two at a time aboard Me 323 Gigant transports to Schwechat for final assembly.

Von Loßberg was also involved in a 'fly-off' between a Ju 188 (flown by himself) and an He 219 piloted by NJG 1's Major Streib, which took place on 25–26 March. Inclusion of the Ju 188 (which did not exist in a nightfighter variant) was the result of the increasingly malevolent interest in the programme being shown by Udet's successor Generaloberst Milch. For whatever reason, Milch was now implacably opposed to the He 219, while at the same time being a staunch proponent of Junkers-produced nightfighters.

Unfortunately for Milch, the 'fly-off' and its associated evaluation proved that the He 219 was 25 to 40 km/h faster than the Ju 188, displayed

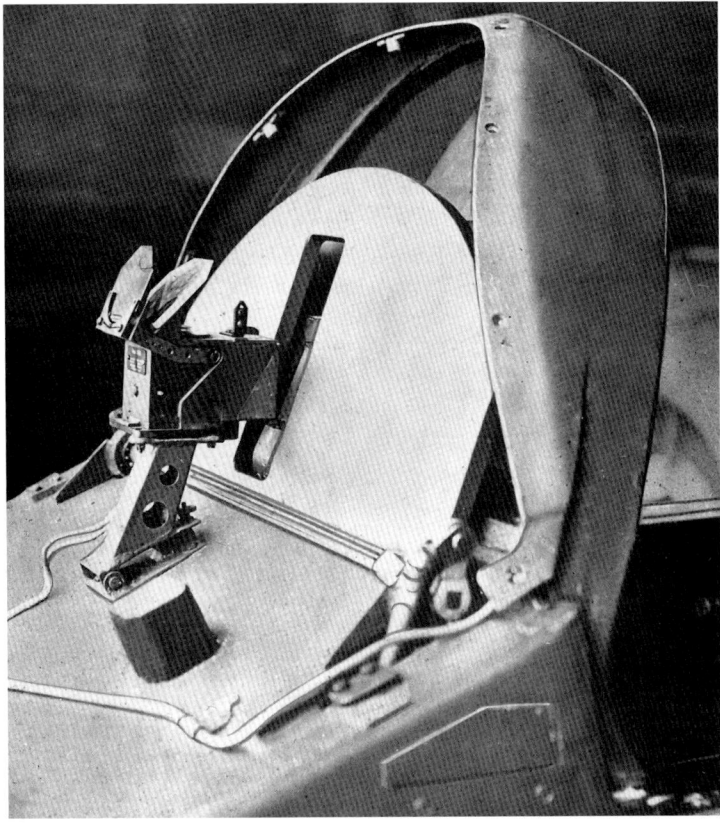

The early He 219s incorporated the curious fold-down armour plate shown here which, when in the upright position, obscured the pilot's forward view with the exception of a cut out for his *Revi* 16B gunsight. In later aircraft, this arrangement appears to have been superseded by an internal armoured glass windshield that was positioned between the pilot and the curved front of the aircraft's canopy (*EN Archive*)

'more fighter-like' handling characteristics, had evidenced a performance that surpassed estimates during the four months it had been flying and required two-thirds less time to build than the Ju 188.

On 30 May, Kammhuber and Generalmajor Dietrich Peltz (the Luftwaffe's then *Inspekteur der Kampfflieger* [Inspector of Bombers], who was interested in the He 219's potential as a fast bomber) visited Venlo, in the Netherlands, to inspect the He 219 V7. After a 'close examination', both men commented on it 'very favourably'. It was at this point that Kammhuber decided that the He 219's first operational sortie would be flown by the V9.

During May, NJG 1 had received V7 Wk-Nr 190007 G9+DB, V8 Wk-Nr 190008 G9+EB and V9 Wk-Nr 190009 G9+FB for operational evaluation. On the night of 11–12 June, Major Werner Streib and his bordfunker (radio/radar operator), Unteroffizier Helmut Fischer, took off in G9+FB as part of the defence against an RAF Bomber Command raid (numbering 783 aircraft) on Düsseldorf. At 0105 hrs, Streib encountered No 408 Sqn Halifax B II JB792 and shot it down. Twenty-three minutes later, he added a second Halifax B II (JB972, again from No 408 Sqn) to the night's tally, with a third Halifax B II (HR719 of No 158 Sqn) going down at 0155 hrs. Streib destroyed Lancaster B II DS647 of No 115 Sqn 21 minutes later, followed by a fourth unidentified Halifax B II at 0222 hrs.

Breaking off combat, Streib now headed home to Venlo, where he discovered that his aircraft's landing flaps were not functioning and, in the ensuing hard landing, his nightfighter was written off. When the wreck came to a halt, its cockpit section had broken off completely from the rest of its fuselage and its back was broken. Surprisingly, Streib emerged from the crash virtually unscathed, while Fischer suffered arm and leg injuries that put him out of action for the next six weeks. In this way (and in just under two-and-a-half hours), the He 219 made its little short of spectacular combat debut.

Milch's animus towards the Heinkel nightfighter was again demonstrated on 15 June when (and following Streib's extremely successful sortie of just three days earlier) he declared that;

'The He 219 is good, it shot down five in one mission [that of 11–12 June 1943]. I can't ask for more than that. But perhaps Streib would have had just as much success with another machine?'

On 10 July the He 219 V2 crashed (killing its pilot, Flugzeugführer Könitzer), at which time the RLM's production plan 223 (promulgated on 15 April 1943) was calling for a monthly output of 50 He 219s.

On 10 August the He 219 V16 Wk-Nr 190016 was the first of the type to be fitted with FuG 220 airborne intercept (AI) radar in place of the earlier FuG 202/212 equipment. Ten days later, Milch was on the attack again when he stated that the Ju 188 was at least as good a nightfighter as the He 219. On what basis this conclusion was arrived at is unclear, as a nightfighter variant of the Junkers aircraft did not (and would never) exist.

At around the same time, Streib is reported to have described the He 219 as becoming too heavy and 'clumsy' – a view (if truly reported) which

Forward hemisphere crew protection was provided by the armoured assembly seen here that formed the front of the cockpit bath (*EN Archive*)

would certainly have been grist to Milch's anti-He 219 mill. That the addition of operational equipment affected the aircraft's performance is a given, as illustrated by the introduction of exhaust flame dampers that reduced its maximum speed by 18 km/h.

Milch's opposition failed to prevent the start of quantity production of the He 219 (at Rostock-Marienehe) on 3 August. At this remove, his obsession with the Ju 188 as a nightfighter is hard to understand, bearing in mind (as already noted) that no such aircraft ever materialised. More comprehensible is the He 219 programme's virtually continual quest for better speed performance. In this context, late September 1943 saw the BMW 003 turbojet-equipped He 219A-010 Wk-Nr 190060 (also variously known as the He 219A-010/TL and the He 219 V17) achieve a speed of 539 km/h at sea level. While this was an improvement over the standard aircraft's performance, the idea of an auxiliary jet engine was not pursued due to its impact on handling.

During October 1943, Heinkel's technical field service team was reporting that the He 219s at Venlo were encountering problems with leaking fuel tanks. By 1 December, Schwechat had delivered 30 He 219s, a figure that probably included a number of true prototypes (aside from A-0 aircraft that were used for trials, and as such were given prototype numbers). Planned He 219 production now stood at 1,093 examples, with Mielec acting as a subcontractor on the programme. Again, 183 He 219A-0 aircraft were to be built at Rostock-Marienehe, where 715 He 219A-1s (see Chapter Two) were to follow. A further 165 He 219A-0s were to be produced at Schwechat, a figure that might rise to 195 examples.

With Kammhuber now out of the nightfighting picture (as a result of his fall from grace in the wake of the RAF's first use of the *Window* radar countermeasure during July 1943), December 1943 saw Milch again try to halt He 219 production and to switch Heinkel to participation in a Junkers nightfighter programme. Three proposals were tabled at this time as follows – He 219 production should be wound down and Heinkel's Group North facilities should be switched to Ju 88G production, with its South Group switching to the Do 335 programme; He 219 production should be immediately reduced from 100 to 50 machines per month (to be built by the company's South Group), with the North Group to produce 50 Ju 88Gs per month; no more than 100 He 219s should be built per month. At this point the Ju 88G was still under development and no nightfighter prototype of the Do 335 had been produced.

On the other side of the coin, 13 December 1943 saw the Luftwaffe's *General der Jagdflieger*, Oberst Adolf Galland, request a high-altitude version of the He 219 powered by DB 603G engines (with GM-1 power boost) and armed with a pair of 30 mm MK 108 cannon mounted in an oblique, upward-firing *Schräge Musik* (strange or jazz music) installation.

During the same month, discussions were held concerned with finding a name for the He 219, with *Marder* (Marten, a weasel-like creature of the *genus* Martes), *Herkules* and *Hermes* all being proposed. None found favour, so the He 219 remained the He 219, with the often-quoted *Uhu* name NEVER becoming the type's official title.

April 1944 saw yet another attempt to stop production of the He 219. This latest attack was based on the 'fact' that the frontline units did not want the type. Heinkel's Generaldirektor Dr Freydag fired off an immediate telex to the RLM drawing attention to the favourable comments on the He 219 made by NJG 1's Technical Officer Oberleutnant Hausdorf, nightfighter pilots Major Rudolf Schönert and Hauptmann Ernst-Wilhelm Modrow, Generalmajor Joseph 'Beppo' Schmidt (commander of 1. *Jagdkorps*) and Major Gerd Müller-Trimmbusch ('Galland's right hand man'). Freydag also noted that Müller-Trimmbusch had commented unfavourably on Focke-Wulf's Ta 154, which was another potential contender to the He 219, and whose design had begun in late 1942.

Irrespective of the ongoing machinations, He 219A-0 production at Schwechat was halted on 23 April 1944 when the site (and others in the Vienna area) was the subject of a heavy attack by 143 B-24 Liberator bombers from the Fifteenth Air Force of the United States Army Air Forces (USAAF). According to USAAF records, this raid 'almost totally destroyed' Schwechat's main assembly hall, 'gutted' three hangers and 'badly damaged' a fourth. Modern research suggests that the bombing destroyed five He 219s (Wk-Nrs 190225, 190227, 190230, 190231 and 190232).

Elsewhere, on 25 May 1944, Reichsmarschall Hermann Göring, Commander-in-Chief of the Luftwaffe, decreed that development and construction of the He 219 should stop in favour of the Ju 388, citing raw materials availability as the reason for the decision. On 13 June this decision was overturned at what must have been something of a tense meeting. Here, Karl-Otto Saur (head of the *Reich*'s *Jägerstab* production organisation) enquired why the He 219 should be cancelled given its successes. Stabsingenieur Walter Baist (from the Rechlin test centre) replied that the frontline units preferred the Ju 388, at which point, Heinkel's Dr Freydag pointed out that the Ju 388 was not yet operational.

Quite why Baist made this statement remains unclear, and after 'lengthy debate', the He 219 was reinstated and was to be 'immediately' fitted with an improved DB 603 engine that would enable it to better counter the RAF's Mosquito bomber, fighter and reconnaissance aircraft. The anti-Mosquito role was deemed to be of the greatest importance, and although the He 219 was the Luftwaffe's fastest nightfighter, it was unable

As a nightfighter, the He 219 had a forward-firing armament of up to six assorted 20/30 mm cannon. Shown here are one of the blast tubes which served the aircraft's pair of wing-mounted weapons (left) and the ventral fairing (right) that housed up to four such weapons (*EN Archive*)

to match the speed and altitude performance of the Mosquito except on relatively rare occasions. As for the installation of improved DB 603 engines, this seems never to have been carried through.

As a result of the 23 April raid, Schwechat (which was slated to complete a production run of 120 He 219A-0s) stopped building the A-0 at airframe 106, with the remaining aircraft parts being moved to the He 219 repair facility at Cheb, in what was then German-occupied Czechoslovakia. More damage to the programme was inflicted by the USAAF on 8 July when Heinkel's Zwölfaxing plant in Austria was hit, causing its work to be transferred to the now repaired Schwechat site, which was already near full capacity producing the He 219 and being slated for production of the He 162 jet fighter.

On a brighter note, the end of June 1944 saw the completion of the development and testing of the He 219's ejector seat, with maximum speeds and altitudes for safe ejection being established as 550 km/h at 1000 m, 620 km/h at 4000 m and 780 km/h at 8000 m. The following month the RLM issued a contract for the construction of 20 He 219s powered by the 1726 hp Junkers Jumo 213E. With these engines, the He 219 was expected to be able to reach a speed of 640 km/h at 9500 m. At the time of the award, five prototypes of what became known as the He 219D-1 were already under construction.

By the mid-summer of 1944, He 219 production (at the rate of five aircraft per month) had restarted at Schwechat, with mid-July seeing the plant being instructed to switch from the He 219A-2 to the A-5. In the event, the A-5 was never produced at Schwechat. Stepping back slightly, in late June He 219A-2 production had commenced at Rostock-Marienehe – a process preceded by a test run of 15 He 219A-0s.

The USAAF struck again when, on 4 August, the Britain-based Eighth Air Force bombed Rostock-Marienehe. Some 60 per cent of the works area at the northern Germany plant was reported to have been hit and the raid as a whole was said to have damaged five and destroyed two He 219s. Of the damaged aircraft, Wk-Nr 290016 was scrapped.

During the same month, the approach of the Red Army caused He 219 work at Mielec to cease, with the factory's machinery and equipment being moved to Gandersheim in central Germany. It has also been suggested that He 219 fuselage construction may have been moved from Mielec to Barth in northeastern Germany. Of the He 219s that were being produced, the period June–September 1944 saw 34 aircraft placed in storage (possibly at Welzow, in eastern Germany) rather than being issued to frontline units. Many of these came out of storage during the following November when 44 He 219s were delivered to I./NJG 1 at Münster-Handorf in western Germany (see Chapter Three).

He 219 production at Schwechat came to an end during the last quarter of 1944 as the plant switched over to the He 162 programme. In more detail, the factory had delivered its first five He 219A-2s during September 1944, followed by a further ten aircraft before the line was shut down. Its final five A-2s were converted to Jumo 213-powered He 219D-1s, the only aircraft of the type to be built.

Schwechat's closure was not the end of the story, for Rostock-Marienehe continued to produce He 219A-2s until November 1944, when it switched over to the He 219A-7 model. Even as late as December 1944, *Lieferplan* (delivery schedule) 227/1 was calling for the production of 50 He 219s per month – a figure that was not to be achieved, for January 1945 saw the issuing of an order to terminate propeller-driven nightfighter production. At this point, the building of He 219s was to end when current outstanding orders were completed. This appears to have occurred during the following March.

When the war ended in May 1945, modern research suggests (but does not confirm) that between 268 and 338 He 219s were produced between November 1942 and March 1945. In the first instance, 195 of the 268 are reported to have been delivered to operational units of the Luftwaffe, while Wk-Nr analysis suggests that of the posited 338, Rostock-Marienehe built 201, with Schwechat producing the remaining 137.

Within these totals, Schwechat is credited with having produced 11 prototypes (Wk-Nrs 190002–190012, built between January–June 1943), 106 He 219A-0s (Wk-Nrs 190051–190075, 190097–190131, 190175–190194 and 190210–190235, built between July 1943 and June 1944), 15 He 219A-2s (Wk-Nrs 420319–420333, built between August–December 1944) and five He 219D-1s (Wk-Nrs 420371–420375, built between January–March 1945).

Comparable figures for Rostock-Marienehe have been given as the He 219 V1 (Wk-Nr 219001, built in November 1942), 15 He 219A-0s (Wk-Nrs 210901–210905 and 211116–211125, built between March–June 1944), 85 He 219A-2s (Wk-Nrs 290001–290020, 290054–290078, 290110–290129 and 290186–290205, built between July–November 1944) and 100 He 219A-7s (Wk-Nrs 310106–310115, 310181–310230 and 310311–310350, built between December 1944 and March 1945). As already suggested, these figures are best viewed as provisional – a situation which is particularly true for the He 219A-7.

A near head-on view of the He 219 V8 Wk-Nr 190008 DH+PX as it appeared at an aircraft display at the Rechlin test centre on 3 September 1943. Note the aircraft's four-bladed propellers and overall *Farbton 76 lichtblau/graublau* (light blue/grey blue, RLM 76) colouration, which almost certainly was applied over an original overall RLM 22 *schwarz* (black) scheme. The aircraft's FuG 202 AI radar array, early style of wing leading edge air intakes and the sheer size of the beast are emphasised from this angle. The He 219 V8 gives a good impression of the configuration of the three examples that were delivered to NJG 1 for operational testing in May 1943 (*EN Archive*)

CHAPTER TWO

INTO COMBAT

As recounted in Chapter One, *General der Flieger* Josef Kammhuber (in his capacity as *Kommandierender General* of the Luftwaffe's nightfighting XII *Fliegerkorps*) was a staunch advocate for the He 219. Indeed, he was instrumental in the decision to deliver the He 219 V7, allocated the *Verbandekenzeichen* (unit code) G9+DB, V8 G9+EB and V9 G9+FB to NJG 1 for operational trials during May 1943.

At the same time, Kammhuber wished to see a *Gruppe* of 20 to 30 such aircraft in service by no later than April of the following year. Of the three, the He 219 V8 was transferred to the Rechlin test centre for undercarriage tests, leaving I./NJG 1's *Stab* (staff) flight with just two aircraft with which to carry out the programme. It was one of these that Major Streib used to make the He 219's first operational sortie on 11–12 June 1943 (as detailed in the caption accompanying the cover artwork). While racking up an impressive five victories, the end of this 2 hr 24 min sortie saw G9+FB written off, leaving the *Gruppe* with just a single airworthy He 219.

The remaining aircraft (He 219 V7 G9+DB) next appears in action on the night of 16–17 June when I./NJG 1 claimed 22 victories during an RAF raid on Köln. Among the *Gruppe*'s response was the He 219 V7 flown by Hauptmann Hans-Dieter Frank and his bordfunker, Feldwebel Erich Gotter. On 1 July Frank became I./NJG 1's *Kommandeur* when Streib with promoted to the position of NJG 1's *Kommodore*.

At the end of his epic sortie of 11–12 June 1943, Major Streib's He 219 was written off in a hard landing at Venlo (*EN Archive*)

OVERLEAF
The aircraft's nose section broke away from its fuselage during the incident on 11–12 June 1943. Indeed, Streib and his bordfunker, Unteroffizier Helmut Fischer, were lucky to have escaped with their lives bearing in mind the near destruction of their aircraft (*Chris Goss Collection*)

On 24 July, the He 219 V12 was delivered to NJG 1, where it joined the He 219 V10 which had been allocated the V9's old *Verbandekenzeichen* G9+FB. The following night, Frank was again airborne aboard G9+FB in opposition to a raid on Essen. During this sortie, he claimed No 50 Sqn Lancaster B III ED753 destroyed at 0056 hrs, followed by No 429 Sqn Wellington B X HE803 at 0130 hrs. Both these aircraft were shot down during a *Himmelbett* (four-poster bed) ground-controlled interception (GCI) patrol.

Three nights later, *Stab* I./NJG 1's Hauptmann Manfred Meurer (a very successful He 219 pilot of whom, more later) is reported to have shot down an RAF Mosquito while flying a Bf 110G. This was only the fifth Mosquito claim of the war to date made by the *Nachtjagdverband* (the Luftwaffe's nightfighter arm).

On 12 August, the RLM reported that He 219A-01 (Wk-Nr 190051), A-03 (Wk-Nr 190053), A-04 (Wk-Nr 190054), A-05 (Wk-Nr 190055), A-06 (Wk-Nr 190056) and A-07 (Wk-Nr 190057) had been assigned to NJG 1 at Venlo, with all bar the He 219A-01 having 'complete' FuG 220 AI radar installations in place of the earlier FuG 202/212 equipment. Three days later, the He 219 V10 was 20 per cent damaged when it made a belly landing at Venlo, while on the night of 23–24 August, Hauptmann Frank used the He 219 V12 to shoot down No 207 Sqn Lancaster B III ED550 at 2340 hrs.

On the last night of August, 660 RAF bombers struck Mönchengladbach and Rheydt. These raids allowed Frank to increase his score by two when (again, at the controls of the He 219 V12) he destroyed Stirling B III EF438 of No 149 Sqn at 0318 hrs, followed by No 432 Sqn Wellington B X JA118 at 0330 hrs. During this sortie Frank's aircraft was hit by defensive fire from one of his victims, and he was forced to return to base on a single engine. Typical of the mythology that has built up around the He 219 since May 1945, it is claimed that during the same sortie Frank shot down a third aircraft (a Lancaster) while flying on one engine! It hardly needs to be stated that modern research has not confirmed this.

Oberstleutnant Werner Streib was a great advocate for the He 219, and he was the first to prove the type's potential as a nightfighter. Streib became involved in nightfighting when he was appointed *Staffelkapitän* of 2./NJG 1 on 26 June 1940. Thereafter, he rose through the ranks to become an Oberstleutnant on 1 May 1944. Between June 1940 and May 1945, his career included command of NJG 1's I. *Gruppe* and then of NJG 1 itself. On 16 March 1944, he was appointed the Luftwaffe's *Inspekteur der Nachtjagd*. During his nightfighting career, Streib is credited with one daylight and 64 night victories, together with another kill which remained unconfirmed at war's end (*Public Domain*)

As autumn set in, 2 September saw He 219A-01 and A-03 issued to I./NJG 1, and it is suggested that these two aircraft were the first to be received by the unit equipped for the FuG 220 *Lichtenstein* SN 2 radar.

In terms of operations, 5–6 September saw the He 219 V10 and V12 airborne against RAF bombing raids on Mannheim and Ludwigshafen (opposite each other on the banks of the upper Rhine). Of the two, the He 219 V12 was being flown by Hauptmann Frank, while the V10 was piloted by Oberleutnant Heinz Strüning in his capacity as 3./NJG 1's *Staffelkapitän*. During the sortie, Frank claimed Lancaster B III JB133 of No 619 Sqn (shot down at 0015 hrs), while the He 219 V10 was hit by defensive fire from a bomber it was attacking. The damage inflicted was bad enough to cause Strüning and his bordfunker, Oberfeldwebel Willi Bleier, to bail out of their crippled aircraft. Neither Strüning's nor Bleier's ejector seats worked, so both had to exit the aircraft 'conventionally'. Strüning was injured whilst doing so, and Bleier perished when he struck the He 219's tail assembly.

On the night of 22–23 September, Hannover was the target for the RAF's 'heavies'. In response, NJG 1 scrambled two He 219s, two Ju 88s and seven Bf 110s at 2130 hrs for a *Zahme Sau* (literally, tame sow but more usually translated as tame boar) pursuit nightfighting operation. At this stage in the war, the *Nachtjagdverband* crews have been described as being neither 'comfortable nor familiar' with the new *Zahme Sau* technique that was beginning to supersede the earlier *Himmelbett* style of GCI nightfighting.

The following night, Mannheim was the target of a force of 620 RAF bombers. NJG 1 scrambled two He 219s, four Bf 110s and a Ju 88 in response, with the aircraft being fed into the bomber 'stream' from nightfighter beacon *Ida*. Of the pair of He 219s, one was flown by *Stab* I./NJG 1's Leutnant Walter Shön, while the other appears to have been piloted by Hauptmann Frank. Shön claimed No 78 Sqn Halifax B II LW266 at 2253 hrs, with Frank accounting for No 75 Sqn Stirling B III EH936 at 2330 hrs.

This was to be Frank's last victory, for on 27–28 September (during a raid on Hannover, which was opposed by his He 219, together with three Do 217s, 34 Ju 88s and 137 Bf 110s) he and his bordfunker, Oberfeldwebel Erich Gotter, were killed when their He 219A-0 Wk-Nr 190053 G9+CB collided with another German nightfighter while being attacked by an RAF Beaufighter flown by No 141 Sqn's CO, and high-scoring ace, Wg Cdr J R D 'Bob' Braham. Frank ejected from his doomed aircraft but was strangled by his helmet's radio lead, which he had failed to disconnect prior to ejecting, while Gotter attempted a 'conventional' bail out and was found dead on the ground several days later.

Frank was replaced in the role of I./NJG 1 *Kommandeur* by Hauptmann Meurer, who was recalled from II./NJG 5, to whom he had been recently posted from 3./NJG 1 as *Gruppenkommandeur*.

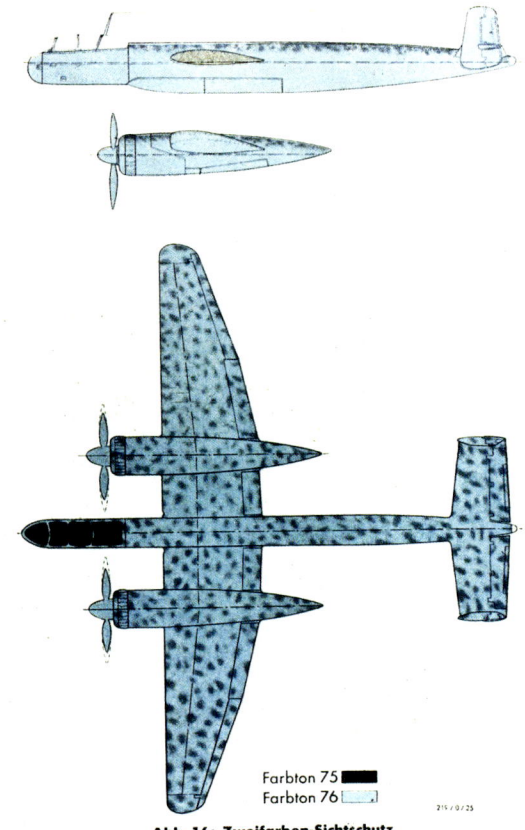

Abb. 16: Zweifarben-Sichtschutz

Farbton 75
Farbton 76

When NJG 1 began to receive more He 219s, the type adopted an RLM 75 *grauviolett* (violet grey)/RLM 76 colour scheme of the type shown in this He 219A-0 manual illustration. While this scheme remained constant throughout the aircraft's career, different interpretations of it abounded, resulting in the considerable variation in finishes seen in many photographs of the type. This was further blurred by late-war applications of RLM 81 *dunkelbraun* (dark brown) and RLM 82 *olivgrün* (olive green) to enhance ground concealment, starboard wing undersurfaces in RLM 22 for ground-to-air identification and complete RLM 22 undersurfaces applied to those aircraft falling within the Wk-Nrs 290057–290126 range (*EN Archive*)

Wg Cdr Bob Braham (right), seen here with his regular navigator, Flt Lt Bill Gregory (left), in 1944 in front of a No 613 Sqn Mosquito FB VI, inflicted an early blow on I./NJG 1's He 219 operations when he was involved in the death of the unit's *Gruppenkommandeur*, and 51-victory ace, Hauptmann Hans-Dieter Frank, on 27–28 September 1943. Frank and his bordfunker, Oberfeldwebel Erich Gotter, were killed when their He 219A-0 Wk-Nr 190053 G9+CB collided with a Bf 110G nightfighter while being attacked by an RAF Beaufighter flown by fellow ace Wg Cdr Braham, who was then CO of No 141 Sqn (*Public Domain*)

The month ended with a raid on Bochum on the night of 29–30 September that was opposed by a single He 219, 85 Bf 110s and 26 Ju 88s. It is also worth noting that Hauptmann Meurer had almost lost his life in September 1943 too, only avoiding certain death when he recovered from a stall while flying the He 219 V7 at 'low altitude'. This alarming incident probably took place while Meurer was converting from the Bf 110 to the He 219.

On 1 October, I./NJG 1 reported that the He 219 V12 and He 219A-01 were available for frontline operations, with the He 219 V7 being used as a trainer and as an instructional airframe. By the end of the month the *Gruppe* had received He 219A-04, A-05, A-06, A-07 and A-09, bringing its complement of Heinkel nightfighters to eight. By 13 October there were seven He 219s at Venlo, two of which were serviceable. Use of the He 219 V7 as a trainer is attested to by Hauptmann Modrow and his bordfunker, Gefreiter Erich Schneider, logging 11 such flights in the aircraft between 14–22 October. At this point, obtaining fuel for training sorties was clearly not the problem that it was to become over the next 17 months. The availability of additional aircraft also meant that the He 219 could enter *Staffel* service with I./NJG 1 rather than just with the *Gruppe*'s *Stab*.

On the operational front, the night of 1–2 October saw one of the *Gruppe*'s He 219s scrambled to oppose an RAF raid on Hagen, in western Germany, while on 18–19 October the *Stab*'s Hauptmann Meurer claimed No 103 Sqn Lancaster B III JB279 at 2003 hrs. Here, the 'heavies' were attacking Hannover, and Meurer's victim collided with another Lancaster in the strike force. Although two four-engined bombers were involved in the incident, Meurer only claimed one.

Two days later, Leutnant Shön and his bordfunker, Unteroffizier Georg Marotzke, were killed when their He 219A-04 (Wk-Nr 190054) crashed

While the He 219 may have had difficulty in intercepting RAF Mosquitos, it was a fearsome heavy bomber killer, with many Lancasters (a No 50 Sqn example is shown here – the unit lost at least three Lancasters to He 219s) falling to its battery of anywhere up to six forward-firing cannon (*Author's Collection*)

at Storbeck, some 20 km northwest of Stendal, in central Germany. The cause of the crash remains unknown, and both men ejected from their stricken fighter, with their bodies being found near their ejector seats in the Osterburg (then Klein Batterstedt) suburb of Stendal.

On 20–21 October, a *Zahme Sau* He 219 sortie contributed to the defence of Leipzig, while Hauptmann Meurer scored his second He 219 victory of the month the following night when he destroyed No 61 Sqn Lancaster B I W4357 during a raid on Hannover. This kill was achieved in bad weather, and Meurer and his bordfunker, Oberfeldwebel Gerhard Scheibe, were part of a force of two He 219s, two Ju 88s and seven Bf 110s that NJG 1 scrambled at 2130 hrs for *Zahme Sau* patrols. The following night the *Geschwader* launched two He 219s, four Bf 110s and a Ju 88 on another *Zahme Sau* operation against an attack on Mannheim, in southwest Germany.

As already noted, these early *Zahme Sau* sorties were not particularly successful, as the crews required time to become familiar with, and to master, the new technique.

To round off the month, RAF Bomber Command returned to German skies on the night of 27–28 October when the 'heavies' struck at Hannover. Again, Hauptmann Frank's He 219 was one of the Luftwaffe nightfighters that opposed this attack.

On 2 November, NJG 1 received He 219A-011 Wk-Nr 190061 from the Berlin suburb of Diepensee, where the Telefunken company had been calibrating its FuG 220 AI radar. Later in the month, He 219A-012 Wk-Nr 190062 was also delivered to the *Geschwader* at Venlo. Aside from these receipts, November 1943 was not a good month for the He 219, with the type being grounded on the 5th due to a rash of leaking fuel tanks, heating and canopy demisting problems, frozen armoured windscreens at high altitude and unreliable AI radars. These problems were exacerbated by an inability to obtain spare parts (with the exception of tyres), resulting in NJG 1 having to cannibalise aircraft to maintain an operational He 219 capability. Over and above the foregoing, NJG 1 was also requesting master-slave compasses for its Heinkels.

Regarding the SN 2 radar (and as of 5 November 1943), the *Nachtjagdverband* had received 42 such sets, with the FuG 220 as a whole being deemed to be still in the 'developmental stage' due to failures being experienced 'during one in every three take offs'. Of the aircraft fitted with

Ernst-Wilhelm Modrow began his nightfighting career during October 1943 when he was assigned to I./NJG 1. As a Hauptmann, he was appointed *Staffelkapitän* of 1./NJG 1 on 1 April 1944 and is known to have ejected from He 219 *Verbandekenzeichen* G9+HH on 1 February 1945. During the course of 109 sorties as a nightfighter pilot, Modrow was credited with 28 confirmed and five unconfirmed victories (*Chris Goss Collection*)

the radar, only 12 were operational, and there was a 'critical shortage' of electronic filters and specialist technicians to service them.

In order to try to alleviate the situation, several of NJG 1's He 219s (including G9+NK, which was flown in by Hauptmann Modrow and future Knight's Cross recipient Gefreiter Schneider – a rare award for a bordfunker) were sent to the Rechlin test centre for 'essential remedial' work.

With regard to November 1943 operations, the night of 3–4 November saw Hauptmann Meurer score his third He 219 success when he destroyed No 77 Sqn Halifax B II JD321 at 2015 hrs over the Netherlands. The bomber was part of a raid on Düsseldorf, and Meurer's sortie was the only He 219 *Zahme Sau* patrol of the night.

Just under two weeks later, RAF Bomber Command attacked Ludwigshafen on the upper Rhine, with the raid being opposed by one He 219, seven Ju 88s and 19 Bf 110s under 3. *Jagddivision* control. The same command launched a single He 219, eight Ju 88s and 17 Bf 110s (all fitted with FuG 220 *Lichtenstein* SN 2 AI radar) against RAF 'heavies' which attacked Berlin and Stuttgart on the night of 26–27 November. Operations on the nights of 17–18 and 26–27 November both employed the *Zahme Sau* technique.

Hauptmann Meurer's kill on 3–4 November was to be the last victory scored by an He 219 during 1943. Interestingly, this was not his final success of the year, for he downed No 105 Sqn Mosquito B IV DZ354 on the night of 12–13 December at 1925 hrs. On this occasion, he was flying a 'specially prepared' SN 2-equipped Ju 88R-2 nightfighter, and the victory was the only successful result of a 60-sortie serial of anti-Mosquito missions flown by aircraft of the Luftwaffe's I. *Jagdkorps* during the month.

I. *Jagdkorps* had been formed from the service's existing XII *Fliegerkorps* and *Luftwaffenbefehlshaber Mitte* (Air Force Commander Centre) commands on 15 September 1943, and it was in turn subsumed into *Luftflotte Reich* (Air Fleet Germany) at a later date.

As a fall out from the technical problems encountered by NJG 1's He 219s during November 1943, December saw the *Geschwader* introduce a more stringent flight test regime for the type. Now, before an aircraft was accepted for service, it had to undergo engine, SN 2, radio communications/navigation equipment and FuG 101 altimeter functionality checks, together with an assessment of the particular machine's handling characteristics at an altitude of 2000 m prior to acceptance. In more detail, the engine test involved climbing the aircraft to 7000 m at full power, while the radio check encompassed FuG 10 and FuG 16 communications radio operability, 'low frequency air-to-ground'

Hauptmann Manfred Meurer began his nightfighting career when he was assigned to 9./NJG 1 during January 1941. Two years later (as an Oberleutnant), he was appointed as the *Staffelkapitän* of 3./NJG 1, a command he held until 5 August 1943. Thereafter, he was promoted to *Kommandeur* of III./NJG 5, a post he held until he was recalled to NJG 1, where he became (as a Hauptmann) *Kommandeur* of I./NJG 1 on 28 September 1943. Still in post, Meurer was killed in action when his He 219A-0 was in collision with an RAF bomber in the Magdeburg area on the night of 21–22 January 1944. During his career, Meurer is credited with having completed at least 130 combat sorties, during which he claimed 61 confirmed and two unconfirmed victories (*Chris Goss Collection*)

communications and direction-finding system functionality. Evaluation of SN 2 performance took the form of two aircraft practice interceptions, and the FuG 101 radio altimeter was calibrated at altitudes down to 200 m.

While the foregoing might have helped with He 219 serviceability, December 1943 saw NJG 1 actually losing aircraft when He 219A-01, A-05, A-07 and one other (possibly A-09 Wk-Nr 190059) were transferred out to *Eprobung* (test) units, leaving the *Geschwader* with just three examples at the end of the month.

Reviewing the type's performance over the period 11–12 June 1943 to the end of December, it proved impossible to field more than single figure numbers of aircraft on any given mission, and classing the type as 'operational' was probably somewhat optimistic. Nonetheless, these 'penny packet' sorties had resulted in 16 victories that were confirmed by the RLM's claims commission. Sadly, for the Luftwaffe, none of these were the seemingly invulnerable RAF Mosquitos which it had been hoped that the He 219's performance would allow it to successfully intercept.

CHAPTER THREE

A NEW YEAR

A close-up of the nose of He 219A-2 Wk-Nr 290013, which clearly illustrates one way of achieving the RLM 75/76 camouflage applied to the type. Here, a uniform base coat of RLM 75 has been applied to the aircraft's uppersurfaces, over which RLM 76 has been sprayed to achieve a mottled effect. Also of note are the white spirals on the aircraft's black propeller spinners, its lack of exhaust flame dampers and the solid RLM 76 finish applied to the forward sections of its engine cowlings (*EN Archive*)

Following the transfer out of four aircraft during December 1943, I./NJG 1's re-capitalisation commenced in January 1944 with the delivery of no fewer than ten He 219s during the course of the month. Here, the aircraft in question were He 219A-015 Wk-Nr 190065, A-017 Wk-Nr 190067, A-020 Wk-Nr 190070, A-022 Wk-Nr 190072, A-023 Wk-Nr 190073, A-024 Wk-Nr 190074, A-025 Wk-Nr 190075, A-026 Wk-Nr 190076, A-028 Wk-Nr 190099 and A-029 Wk-Nr 190100.

While this influx marked the beginning of the *Gruppe*'s conversion from the Bf 110, the process appears to have badly affected its combat capability, with only 13 victories (five by He 219s) being claimed during the first quarter of 1944, as against 45 during the same quarter of the preceding year.

The first identified operational use of the He 219 in 1944 came on the night of 14–15 January when Hauptmann Modrow and his bordfunker, Gefreiter Schneider, were airborne in He 219A-0 G9+CK as part of the defence against an RAF raid on Braunschweig (also known as Brunswick) in northern Germany. Four nights later, Modrow was again scrambled in He 219A-0 G9+AK to contest an attack on Berlin.

The German capital was again the target on 27–28 January, and Modrow and Schneider were again airborne in G9+AK, completing three *Himmelbett* GCI sorties. Elsewhere that same night, Oberleutnant Werner Baake (2./NJG 1's *Staffelkapitän* and future *Kommandeur* of I./NJG 1) was wounded in action defending Germany when the Bf 110G-4 (G9+ML) he was flying collided with a bomber and crashed near Germünd, 16 km southwest of Aachen on the Franco-German border.

Towards the end of the month tragedy again struck the *Gruppe* when, on the night of 21–22 January, Hauptmann Meurer and his bordfunker, Oberfeldwebel Scheibe, were killed when He 219A-020 Wk-Nr 190070 G9+BB collided with a Lancaster. The nightfighter crashed 20 km east of Magdeburg, in northeastern Germany. On this final sortie, Meurer is known to have destroyed No 77 Sqn Halifax B V LK730 at 2310 hrs. He was succeeded as *Kommandeur* of I./NJG 1 by Hauptmann Paul Förster.

The loss of Meurer together with the He 219's grounding during the previous November combined to see the aircraft being used 'sparingly' during February 1944. On a brighter note, I./NJG 1 received He 219A-027 Wk-Nr 190098, A-031 Wk-Nr 190102, A-033 Wk-Nr 190104, A-036 Wk-Nr 190107 and A-039 Wk-Nr 190110 during the month. This allowed the unit to report a strength of 11 He 219s and 16 Bf 110Gs on the 29th.

Elsewhere, 1 February saw He 219A-011 Wk-Nr 190061 transferred from Venlo to the Rechlin test centre for trials, while on the 23rd, the He 219 V12 was destroyed when the roof of the hanger in which the nightfighter was housed collapsed on it during a raid on Venlo by B-26 Marauder medium bombers of the USAAF's 387th Bombardment Group (BG). At the time of its loss, the V12 bore the *Verbandekenzeichen* G9+FK, which was subsequently reused on another He 219 that was 'extensively photographed' for recognition purposes on 18 April 1944.

The ongoing battle against the RAF's Mosquito bomber/reconnaissance/fighter aircraft (an increasing irritant to the Luftwaffe) resulted in the February 1944 formation of *Eprobungskommando* (Test Command – E.Kdo) Schreckenberger within I./NJG 1 as a specific anti-Mosquito capability. Also known as E.Kdo 410, the detachment was equipped with a mixture of Bf 110, He 219, Ju 88R-2 and Me 410A-1 fighters. During its five-month existence, the unit achieved no victories over its illusive foe.

As was the case in February 1944, the following month saw I./NJG 1 receive additional He 219s (in this case, four Schwechat-produced aircraft, including Wk-Nrs 190103 and 190105, He 219A-032 and A-034, respectively), bringing the *Gruppe*'s inventory to 14 Bf 110Gs, 15 He 219s and a Ju 88R-2 by the end of March.

Identified He 219 combat operations during that month comprised those flown on 24–25 (a raid on Berlin) and 30–31 March – the latter mission was the disastrous attack on Nürnberg (Nuremberg) that cost RAF Bomber Command 95 aircraft. In more detail, the 24–25 March operation saw I./NJG 1 scramble an unknown number of He 219s from Venlo at 2150 hrs, with Oberleutnant Josef Nabrich (of 3./NJG 1) and his bordfunker, Feldwebel Fritz 'Pitt' Habricht, claiming No 44 Sqn Lancaster B I ME672 destroyed at 0030 hrs.

Six nights later, the Modrow/Schneider team (in He 219A-2 G9+CK) shot down two Halifax B IIIs, the first of which (No 640 Sqn aircraft LW500) fell at 0413 hrs. The second (No 158 Sqn aircraft HX322) followed at 0430 hrs. It is perhaps worth noting that Modrow is also reported to have flown G9+CK on an unsuccessful anti-Mosquito *Himmelbett* sortie at some point during March, although the author cannot confirm when this took place.

This wreck (which is said to have been found at Halle during the spring of 1945) is the only He 219A known to the author to have been photographed bearing NJGr 10's 1L identification code. Other shots suggest that it may have been aircraft M of that *Gruppe*'s second *Staffel*. Note the dense uppersurface RLM 81/82 overspray and the odd use of white paint to obscure part of the nightfighter's identification code on its starboard side (*EN Archive*)

April 1944 saw a new departure for the Heinkel nightfighter when He 219A-053 Wk-Nr 190124 was delivered to *Nachtjagdgruppe* (Nightfighter Group – NJGr) 10 at Finsterwalde, in eastern Germany. Formed on 1 January 1944 under the command of high-scoring nighterfighter ace Major Rudolf Schoenert, NJGr 10 undertook nightfighting 'tactics and techniques' trials. The unit survived until April 1945, and at its peak (June 1944) had a strength of ten He 219s alongside an assortment of Bf 109, Bf 110, Fw 190, Ju 88 and Ta 154 fighters. Regarding the He 219, Schoenert is reported to have been 'fulsome in his praise' of the aircraft's speed and handling characteristics.

Elsewhere, I./NJG 1 is credited with 14 victories during April 1944, having by then received 24 new He 219s to allow the unit to complete its conversion from the Bf 110. Indeed, by month-end, the *Gruppe*'s He 219 inventory is reported to have reached 35, plus a lone Ju 88R-2.

Operationally, on 1 April 1944 the Luftwaffe's I. *Jagdkorps* assumed responsibility for all the nightfighters defending the *Reich* except for a small number of units in France that remained under the jurisdiction of II. *Jagdkorps*.

Specific to He 219 operations, on 7–8 April Modrow and his bordfunker Schneider (in He 219A-0 G9+LK) attempted to intercept RAF bombers that were 'Gardening' (dropping sea mines) off the Dutch coast. G9+LK is described as having *bessere zieldarstellung* (better target presentation), which is thought to indicate installation of a FuG 220 AI radar variant that had improved close-range resolution. The earliest SN 2 radars had had to be teamed with FuG 212 equipment to provide adequate close-range coverage.

Moving forward, 10–11 April saw the RAF attacking rail targets in Belgium and France, while a force of 36 Mosquitos bombed Hannover. Elements of I./NJG 1 (including 3. *Staffel*'s Feldwebel Alfred Rauer and his bordfunker, Feldwebel Heinz Weber, in G9+LL) were scrambled from Venlo against the enemy at 2245 hrs.

Rauer and Weber were airborne again the following night (again in G9+LL) as part of the response to an RAF Bomber Command attack on Aachen. During this mission, Rauer claimed No 61 Sqn Lancaster B III JA696 at 2302 hrs. For their part, Oberleutnant Baake and Hauptmann Modrow's usual bordfunker, Gefreiter Schneider, in G9+BK, destroyed No 619 Sqn Lancaster B III EE116 35 minutes later. The next night (11–12 April) was notable for being the date of the first successful ejection from an operational He 219.

The first such escape from any He 219 occurred on 10 July 1943 when Heinkel ingenier Consten successfully evacuated the He 219 V2 (see Chapter One). His pilot, Flugzeugführer Könitzer, was not so lucky, being killed in the incident. The 11–12 April escapees were Unteroffizier Herter and his bordfunker, Gefreiter Werner Perbix, who were almost certainly shot down by the Mosquito NF II of No 239 Sqn ace Flt Lt Nevil Reeves, who claimed a 'Do 217'. Reeves submitted the following combat report after the engagement;

'When seven miles north of Aachen, the navigation lights of an aircraft flying west to east were seen some six to seven miles away at 15,000 ft. [My] Mosquito turned towards it, losing height to 13,000 ft, but the navigation lights were doused. Mosquito continued flying west, and AI contact at 8000 ft was obtained but then lost to interference. Aircraft turned back towards Aachen, climbing to 16,000 ft, and another AI contact [was] obtained [at] maximum range.

'Endeavouring to close in, a further head-on contact [was made] at 14,000 ft and a visual obtained of a Do 217 [sic]. Aircraft fired at 150 yards range and strikes were seen all over enemy aircraft, which immediately burst into flames. Mosquito peeled off to avoid collision. Enemy aircraft blazing fiercely was seen to hit the ground with a spectacular flash. Two parachutes were seen descending into clouds.'

Offsetting the misery of being shot down, Herter and Perbix were each awarded the not insubstantial sum of 1000 *Reichsmarks* by Heinkel for having survived the ejection.

On 22–23 April, I./NJG 1 was in action again as part of the response to RAF raids on Düsseldorf, Braunschweig and the marshalling yards at Laon, in northern France. The *Gruppe*'s pilots destroyed five bombers, with Hauptmann Modrow claiming No 7 Sqn Lancaster B III ND353 at 0110 hrs, either Halifax B III LV780 (of No 424 Sqn) or LW633 (of No 425 Sqn) at 0155 hrs and whichever of the two survived the 0155 hrs attack at 0204 hrs. Elsewhere, 2./NJG 1's Major Hans Karlewski and his bordfunker, Unteroffizier Herman, shot down No 431 Sqn Halifax B III MZ514 at 0139 hrs, while Unteroffizier Karl Wildhagen (also from 2./NJG 1) destroyed No 460 Sqn Lancaster B III LM525 at 0145 hrs. These were the first victories credited to Karlewski and Wildhagen.

On 24–25 April the 'heavies' struck Karlsruhe, with both Hauptmann Modrow (in G9+CK) and Oberleutnant Baake (in VK G9+BK) making claims. In order, Modrow's first kill of the night came at 0005 hrs when he destroyed No 100 Sqn Lancaster B III ND328. At 0334 hrs he shot down a second aircraft (No 425 Sqn Halifax B III MZ573), while Baake claimed No 75 Sqn Lancaster B I ME690 at 0114 hrs. On these sorties, Modrow and Baake were accompanied by bordfunkers Schneider and Bettaque, respectively. On the other side of the balance sheet, Feldwebel Werner Fick and his bordfunker, Feldwebel Friedrich Alster, were killed when their He 219 (Wk-Nr 19103 G9+LK) crashed near Osthein in the Rhône Mountains.

On 18 April 1944, 2./NJG 1 He 219A G9+FK was the subject of a series of all-round air-to-air photographs for use in Luftwaffe aircraft recognition manuals. Although not of the best quality, this view shows G9+FK from below and emphasises its RLM 22 black lower starboard wing (a ground-to-air recognition feature) and the heavy exhaust staining generated by Germany's increasing use of synthetic aviation fuel and running an aircraft's engines at maximum power for prolonged periods (*EN Archive*)

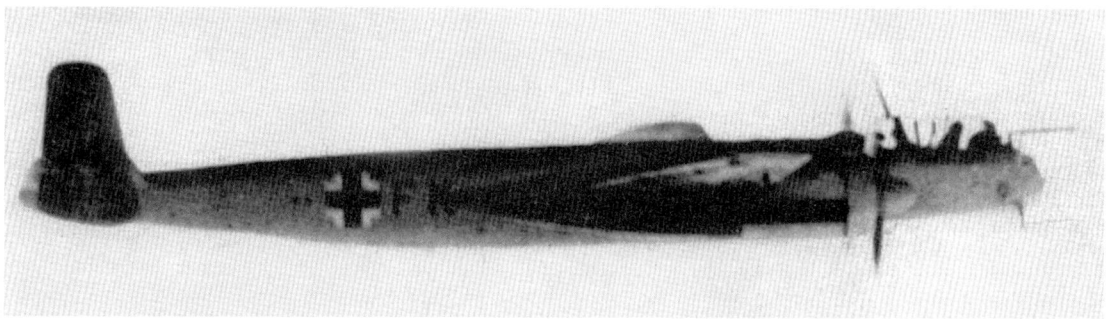

Another photograph from G9+FK's 18 April 1944 air-to-air sortie, this time showing the aircraft side on. Note the *Englandblitz* badge on the nose and its radar equipment, with a dual forward-facing FuG 212/220 nose antenna array. G9+FK was flown on this sortie by future nightfighter ace Hauptmann Ernst-Wilhelm Modrow, who enjoyed notable success in the He 219 between March 1944 and January 1945 (*EN Archive*)

Operations continued apace, with 25–26 April seeing Modrow and Schneider carry out an unsuccessful anti-Mosquito patrol in He 219 V15 Wk-Nr 190064. This aircraft was fitted with the GM-1 power boosting system, and prior to service with I./NJG 1, it is reported to have been used as a testbed for the FuG 16 ZY very high frequency (VHF) transceiver and the FuG 135 *Uhu* guidance transmission device.

The following night, RAF bombers attacked Essen and Schweinfurt, in Germany, and Villeneuve-Saint-Georges in France. I./NJG 1 (including Hauptmann Modrow in G9+GK, 1./NJG 1's Oberleutnant Wilhelm Henseler and 2./NJG 1's Feldwebel Josef Ströhlein) scrambled from Venlo at 0125 hrs. Henseler duly destroyed No 51 Sqn Halifax B III MZ565 at 0158 hrs, followed by Ströhlein's downing of No 10 Sqn Halifax B III HX326 at 0200 hrs.

The month ended with raids on Friedrichshafen, in southern Germany, and rail targets in Aulnoye-Aymeries, in France, and Montzen, in eastern Belgium, on the night of 27–28 April. I./NJG 1 despatched aircraft against (it is assumed) the two northern targets in the 15-minute period between 0105–0120 hrs. During this operation, 1./NJG 1's Oberleutnant Wilhelm Hensler destroyed two Halifax bombers, one at 0202 hrs (unidentified) and the second at 0158 hrs (No 51 Sqn Halifax B III MZ565). Hensler mis-identified one of his victims as having been a Lancaster.

As April 1944 turned into May, the Luftwaffe's use of the He 219 expanded with the delivery of possibly as many as ten aircraft (tentatively identified as Wk-Nrs 190105, 190108, 190109, 190110, 190116, 190118, 190190, 190191, 210902 and 210903) to II./NJG 1 at Sint-Truiden, in Belgium. Six of these are said to have been transfers from I./NJG 1, with the remaining four being factory fresh. Whether or not the four new-builds went to II./NJG 1 remains uncertain, but it is known that Wk-Nr 190116 was lost in a subsequent accident.

In terms of overall inventory, on 1 May I./NJG 1 was able to muster 35 He 219s, with II./NJG 1 having a single such aircraft. By the end of the month, *Stab* NJG 1 had one He 219, I./NJG 1 had 29, II./NJG 1 had seven and 2./NJGr 10 had five – of the latter machines, three have been identified as Wk-Nrs 190051, 190055 and 190057, with the *Stab* aircraft being Wk-Nrs 190189 G9+BA. It is believed that G9+BA was assigned to veteran ace Major Hans-Joachim Jabs (who, as far as is known, never flew it operationally) and to have been transferred to I./NJG 1 on 2 July 1944. Elsewhere, I./NJG 1 is reported to have lost ten He 219s to accidents during the month – a figure that, as of this writing, has not been confirmed.

CHAPTER THREE A NEW YEAR

With regard to combat, the first identified He 219 sorties of the new month came on 1–2 May, when RAF Bomber Command attacked rail targets at Saint-Ghislain and Mechelen, in southwestern and central Belgium, respectively. During these raids, the Modrow/Schneider (in He 219A-2 G9+CK) and Baake/Bettaque (in He 219A-0 G9+BK) crews were airborne, with the former claiming the destruction of No 100 Sqn Lancaster B III ND328 at 0005 hrs. On this occasion, Modrow is reported to have been flying a *Wilde Sau* (literally wild sow, but usually translated as wild boar) freelance patrol.

Five nights later, the Baake/Bettaque crew (in He 219A-0 G9+HK) claimed No 109 Sqn Mosquito B XVI ML985 destroyed at 2335 hrs. The aircraft is described as having been a 'straggler' at an altitude of 8000 m, some 1981 m lower than the rest of its formation. This was almost certainly the first Mosquito victory credited to an He 219 crew, and it appears likely to have been the subject of the gift of ten bottles of Champagne delivered to the crew in acknowledgement of the feat! Baake also claimed to have damaged a B-17 of the Eighth Air Force's 422nd Bombardment Squadron (BS), part of the 305th BG, on the same night – it was rejected by the RLM's claims commission, however.

The Modrow/Schneider crew were also airborne (in G9+CK) on 6–7 May on an unsuccessful *Moskito jagd* (Mosquito hunting) sortie. During daylight on the 7th, Feldwebel Heinzelmann and his bordfunker, Unteroffizier Wilhelm Herling, were killed when their He 219 (Wk-Nr 190115 G9+FH) crashed for reasons unknown at Süchtein, on the Dutch–German border.

I./NJG 1 was back in action on the nights of 8–9 and 10–11 May, with the latter evening seeing the 'heavies' attacking rail targets in Belgium and northern France. Here, He 219s from both I. and II./NJG 1 are reported to have taken off in opposition, with the operation being II./NJG 1's first He 219 patrol. I./NJG 1's aircraft (including G9+RL flown by Feldwebel Alfred Rauer and his bordfunker, Feldwebel Weber) scrambled from Venlo at 2250 hrs for an unsuccessful *Moskito jagd* at 10,000–11,000 m, while II./NJG 1's single He 219 was flown from Deelen, in the Netherlands,

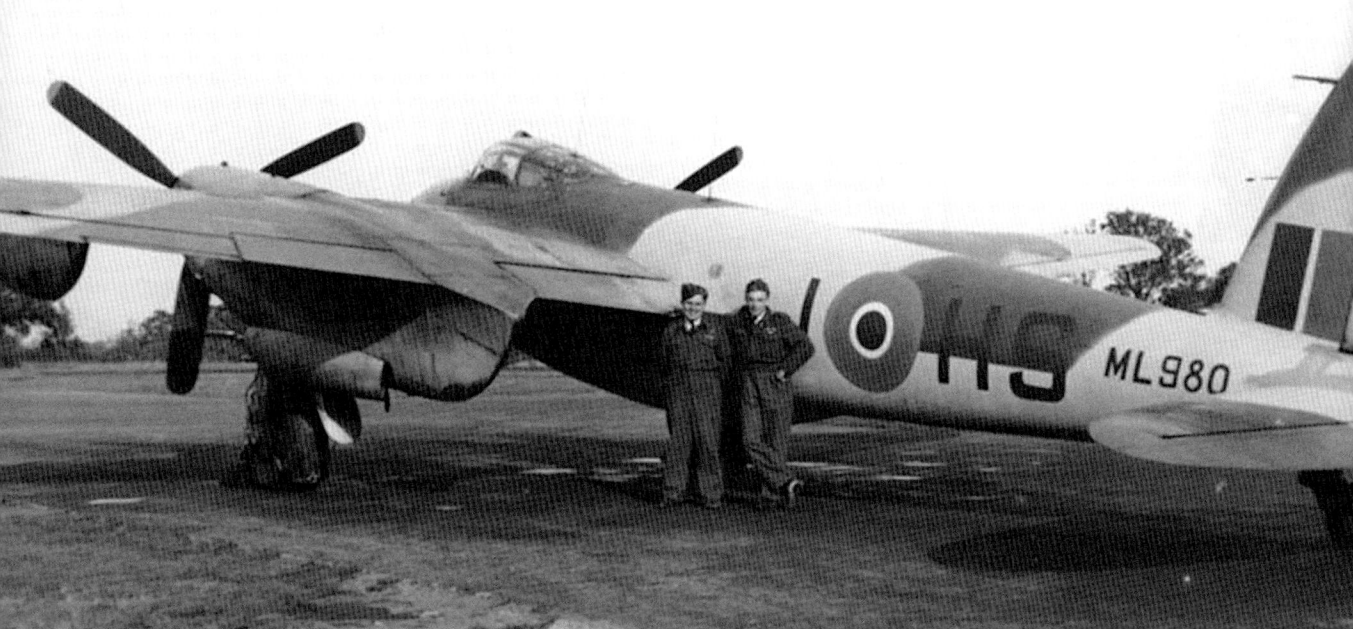

While the He 219 could just about catch a Mosquito B IV bomber, it lacked the speed and altitude capability to be truly effective against the 'wooden wonder', particularly those powered by two-stage Merlin engines. Nevertheless, examples of the de Havilland aircraft fell to the Heinkel nightfighter, with the first Mosquito downed almost certainly being B XVI ML985 of No 109 Sqn on the night of 6–7 May 1944. The aircraft seen in this photograph, ML980, was assigned to the unit at the same time (*Public Domain*)

by Oberleutnant Johannes Hager, who became airborne between 2309–2330 hrs. The *Gruppe* also despatched 11 Bf 110Gs.

In terms of kills, I./NJG 1's Oberleutnant Nabrich claimed No 427 Sqn Halifax B III LV986 as destroyed at 2335 hrs, while the same *Gruppe*'s Hauptmann Strüning was credited with Halifax B III LV985, also from No 427 Sqn, 18 km northeast of Bruges, in Belgium, at 0115 hrs – Strüning identified his victim as being a 'Lancaster'. Despite the RLM confirming the 'kills', both aircraft managed to return home to RAF Leeming, in North Yorkshire, where LV986 was declared a write-off and LV985 was repaired.

On 11–12 May, targets in eastern Belgium (specifically the railway yards at Hasselt and Louvain, together with a military camp at Bourg-Léopold) were attacked. I./NJG 1's Modrow/Schneider crew (in G9+CK) destroyed No 626 Sqn Lancaster B III JB409 at 0026 and No 630 Sqn Lancaster B III ND580 at 0104 hrs, while 2./NJG 1's Oberleutnant Baake accounted for No 103 Sqn Lancaster B III JB733 at 0042 hrs.

The following night, Hasselt and Louvain were again the target for the 'heavies', and I./NJG 1's Modrow (flying He 219A-0 G9+GK), Nabrich and Strüning (in He 219A-0 G9+EL) all claimed kills. In order, Modrow accounted for No 635 Sqn Lancaster B III ND924 at 0002 hrs, followed by No 466 Sqn Halifax B III LV826 at 0100 hrs (both claims were logged as being *anerkannt* [acknowledged] by the RLM). For his part, Nabrich destroyed an unidentified No 640 Sqn Halifax B III at 0020 hrs, while Strüning (3./NJG 1's *Staffelkapitän*) downed No 431 Sqn Halifax B III MZ629 at 0048 hrs.

Nabrich's victory was achieved using an experimental 37 mm BK 3.7 cannon installation, with his bordfunker, Feldwebel Fritz Habicht, noting that the kill was their only success with this upward-firing weapon that literally blew their quarry apart and filled the surrounding sky with flying debris that put Nabrich and Habicht in a 'very tight spot'. Their aircraft (He 219A-0 G9+OL) was badly damaged in the action and only just made it home.

Elsewhere, I./NJG 1's Oberleutnant Baake (in G9+BK) came close to attacking a Bf 110G in a 'friendly fire' incident that illustrates the difficulties of visually identifying aircraft at night.

On 13 May He 219 Wk-Nr 190179 was despatched to Cheb for repairs. Bearing the *Verbandekenzeichen* G9+PK, this aircraft was subsequently assigned to 2./NJG 1 and survived the war. Two days later, the Schwechat-built He 219A-074 Wk-Nr 190188 was delivered to Venlo and assigned to I./NJG 1. It was the first production aircraft to be equipped with the FuG 16 ZY VHF transceiver rather than the FuG 16 ZE model.

Combat was resumed on 19–20 May when the RAF attacked eight tactical targets in France and made a Mosquito strike on Köln. Venlo scrambled its He 219s during the 25-minute period between 2320–2345 hrs on a fruitless *Moskitojagd* against the Köln raiders. Aside from not finding any Mosquitos, II. *Gruppe* had a bad night when Leutnant Otto-Heinrich Fries (II./NJG 1's *technischer Offizier*) and

Shown here in his dress uniform at a funeral, Otto-Heinrich Fries entered the Luftwaffe's nightfighting world during 1942 when he was assigned to I./NJG 1. In August 1943, he was a Feldwebel with 5./NJG 1, and had been promoted to Leutnant by the following October. On 19–20 May 1944, Fries and his bordfunker, Feldwebel Alfred Staffa, successfully ejected from He 219A-0 G9+DC. Serving with 2./NJG 1 and then II./NJG 1 upon his return to operations, Fries had been credited with 17 confirmed night victories by war's end (*Chris Goss Collection*)

his bordfunker, Feldwebel Alfred Staffa, in He 219A-0 G9+DC were shot down by an intruder south of Hertogenbosch, in the Netherlands, at 0125 hrs. Both crewmen ejected safely and without injury from their aircraft (Wk-Nr 190116), which had been assigned to both I. and Stab II./NJG 1, with the latter being referenced by the *Verbandekenzeichen* G9+DC.

During the daylight hours of 21 May, two He 219s engaged on a *Zeidarstellung* (target representation) training flight were intercepted, resulting in the loss of Wk-Nr 190107 G9+FL to an RAF Mosquito FB VI intruder of No 418 Sqn. Unteroffiziere Ewalde Tampke and Eduart Tanbs were both killed in the incident.

Thereafter, 21–22 May saw the beginning of five nights of victories for the He 219s of I./NJG 1. In order, in response to the 21–22 May RAF attack on Duisburg, in northwestern Germany, Hauptmann Strüning (in G9+EL), Oberleutnant Henseler, Hauptmann Modrow (in He 219A-0 G9+EK), Hauptmann Förster and Major Karlewski all claimed victories. In more detail, Strüning destroyed No 460 Sqn Lancaster B I LL951 at 0132 hrs, followed by Henseler downing No 166 Sqn Lancaster B III ND956 five minutes later at 0137 hrs. Modrow weighed in when he destroyed No 635 Sqn Lancaster B III ND819 at 0141 hrs, with Förster claiming No 44 Sqn Lancaster B III ND976 at 0206 hrs – this was Förster's first He 219 victory. I./NJG 1's run of victories that night ended when Major Karlewski destroyed an unidentified Lancaster at 0212 hrs.

The following night, RAF Bomber Command hit Dortmund, with I./NJG 1 racking up five more victories. In time order, Oberleutnant Henseler downed No 103 Sqn Lancaster B III ND629 at 0039 hrs, followed by Major Karlewski claiming No 408 Sqn Lancaster B II LL723 at 0044 hrs. Thirty minutes later, Oberleutnant Baake destroyed No 75 Sqn Lancaster B I ME690 at the same time as Hauptmann Strüning downed No 166 Sqn Lancaster B I LL954. Finally, Hauptmann Modrow (aboard G9+EK) destroyed No 626 Sqn Lancaster B III NE118 at 0125 hrs.

On the night of 24–25 May, the RAF 'heavies' struck at Aachen and I./NJG 1 added five more enemy aircraft to its burgeoning scoreboard for the month. In time order, Major Karlewski downed No 158 Sqn Halifax B III LW720 at 0045 hrs, followed two minutes later by the destruction of No 429 Sqn Halifax B III HX352, credited to Hauptmann Strüning (in G9+EL). At 0241 hrs, Oberleutnant Nabrich downed No 192 Sqn's signals intelligence gathering Halifax B III MZ501. Oberleutnant Henseler claimed No 405 Sqn Lancaster B III ND526 at 0248 hrs, while Hauptmann Strüning destroyed his second aircraft of the night (No 419 Sqn Lancaster B X KB706) at 0251 hrs.

While I./NJG 1's scoring streak continued on 26–27 May with the shooting down of No 692 Sqn Mosquito B IV DZ649 (credited to Feldwebel Rauer and his bordfunker, Feldwebel Weber, in He 219A-0 G9+DL) at 0117 hrs and No 139 Sqn Mosquito B IV DZ610 (by Feldwebel Wilhelm Morlock) at 0127 hrs, it was becoming ever clearer that the He 219 simply did not have the speed or altitude performance to intercept the fast-flying de Havilland twin-engined bombers on a regular basis. The *Nachtjagd*'s Bf 110G-4, Ju 88C-6 and Ju 88G-1 nightfighters had even less chance of overhauling a Mosquito. Morlock's victim, DZ610, may have been 'returning early' from an attack on Ludwigshafen

Two views of the armoured glass screen that replaced the He 219's earlier pilot's fold-down armoured windscreen shield (which drew complaints from frontline pilots), together with the type's forward-facing *Revi* 16B gunsight. Of note is the lack of the starboard side gap between this inner screen and the outer canopy mentioned in the text (*EN Archive*)

1 Revibock
2 Grundplatte für Revibock
3 Schwenkbarer Ösenbolzen mit Rändelschraube
4 Revigrundplatte
5 Gestänge für Sonnenblendscheibe
6 Schubstange für Nachtfilter

Revi 16 B eingebaut

due to 'flight difficulties' that slowed the Mosquito up enough to allow the He 219 to intercept it. The bomber crashed into the North Sea off the Dutch coast.

The final night of the sequence (27–28 May) saw RAF Bomber Command strike multiple targets including the railway yards at Aachen and the military camp at Bourg-Léopold. Overhead the latter site, Feldwebel Morlock, Hauptmann Modrow and Feldwebel Rauer all claimed victories. In the order given, Morlock destroyed a '4-motor' at 0144 hrs (confirmed by the RLM), while Hauptmann Modrow downed No 12 Sqn Lancaster B III ND619 at 0225 hrs, No 101 Sqn Lancaster B III LM459 at 0235 hrs and a third Lancaster (confirmed by the RLM) at 0328 hrs. For his part, Feldwebel Rauer added another Mosquito to his tally when he claimed to have downed B IV DZ423 of No 139 Sqn at 0244 hrs. Although badly damaged, the aircraft made it back to England and crash-landed at RAF Wittering, in Cambridgeshire.

The month ended with a series of raids on tactical targets in France that took place on the night of 31 May/1 June. Again, Modrow filed multiple claims, with the roster this time comprising No 161 Sqn Hudson III V9155 at 0110 hrs and No 138 Sqn Halifax B V LL276 at 0141 hrs. Both of these aircraft were involved in operations in support of the British Special Operations Executive (SOE).

The summer of 1944 probably represented the high-water mark of the He 219's brief combat career. On 1 June 1944, I./NJG 1 is reported to have been able to muster 29 He 219s, with II./NJG 1 having seven, *Stab* NJG 1 one and 2./NJGr 10 five. Elsewhere, NJG 1 received 13 factory-fresh machines during the course of the month. This said, all was not well, for on the 1st He 219 Wk-Nr 190119 G9+AK crashed near Mulbjerge

Hill, in Denmark, during a gunnery training flight. At the time of its loss, G9+AK was carrying a crew of three, with the third member being a ventral observer/gunner. Oberleutnant Friedrich Guth, Feldwebel Andreas Klein and Obergefreiter Herbert Otto were all killed in the incident.

That same day, Heinkel technical engineering staff met representatives of I. and II./NJG 1 at Venlo to discuss ongoing problems with the He 219. Complaints raised included unintentional undercarriage retractions, excessive tyre use, burnt-out brake linings, excessively high oil temperatures (particularly during continuous power climbs to 6000 m) and oil cooler and radiator failures. There were also complaints about the five-week period required to install 30 mm oblique-firing MK 108 *Schräge Musik* weapons. The need for a stronger canopy retaining cable, chaffing of hydraulic lines in the aircraft's nosewheel bay, fuel return line failures, unreliable rubber seals, a poor exhaust flame damper installation, an unreliable hot water cabin heating system and a request to remove the pilot's armoured windscreen shield were issues also raised with Heinkel.

Again, various suggestions were made by the *Gruppen*, which included evaluation of an NJG 1-developed 20 mm MG 151/20 *Schräge Musik* fit and II./NJG 1's ventral gun/observation position. In order, the MG 151/20 *Schräge Musik* featured cannon barrels that were 24 cm shorter than standard, while the II./NJG 1 ventral gun position utilised a 7.92 mm MG 81Z machine gun. Concerning this latter modification, doubts were raised about the shallow angle-of-fire available, together with its potential for affecting the host airframe's compass and centre-of-gravity.

The He 219 returned to combat on 2–3 June when the RAF struck several targets in France. Leutnant Ewald-Werner Hittler of 3./NJG 1 shot down 845th BS/489th BG B-24H 42-94793 in what must be one of the more bizarre air combats of the European war. The particular Liberator had been damaged during a daylight raid on the 2nd and its crew had set it on autopilot and abandoned the bomber. Once over the North Sea, the still-flying aircraft reversed course and re-crossed the Dutch coast, where Hittler attacked it at 2356 hrs. Elsewhere, Hauptman Strüning (in He 219A-0 G9+LK) destroyed No 138 Sqn Halifax B V LL307 at 0036 hrs.

On 3 June, Heinkel's Venlo-based *Technischen Aussendienst* (Technical Field Service) recorded I./NJG 1 as having a total of 31 He 219s, of which 18 were operational, one was having its engines repaired, six were undergoing 'flight operation' work, one was being fitted with a *Schräge Musik* installation, Wk-Nr 190217 was newly delivered and four were on detachment to 'Denmark Command'. Comparable figures for 5 June were 17, 5, 3, 1, 6 and 4, respectively.

Returning to combat operations, on 3–4 June Hauptmann Heinz Eicke and his bordfunker, Oberfeldwebel Heinz Gall, were shot down while flying He 219 Wk-Nr 190188 G9+BL. With an uncontrollable engine fire to deal with, Eicke ejected successfully but Gall was killed. G9+BL crashed near Wilhelminadorp, in the Netherlands, having fallen victim to No 219 Sqn's Plt Off Desmond Tull in Mosquito NF XVII HK248. Ironically, bearing in mind the number of Tull's squadron, it is thought that Wk-Nr 190188 was the first He 219 to be shot down by an RAF nightfighter. Indeed, it took much head scratching before it was actually identified as a Heinkel. Elsewhere, He 219 Wk-Nr 190105 was 25 per cent damaged when its nosewheel collapsed upon landing, with Unteroffizier Heinz Filipzig of 4./NJG 1 being injured in the incident.

Two nights later, Hauptmann Strüning claimed No 515 Sqn Mosquito FB VI NS950 destroyed at 0203 hrs, while He 219A-0 Wk-Nr 190177 G9+IK was lost to an engine fire and crashed eight kilometres east of Herning, in the Netherlands. The aircraft was being flown by Leutnant Ernst Mauss and his bordfunker, Unteroffizier Günther Krause, at the time. The pilot successfully ejected but the bordfunker was killed.

On 10–11 June RAF Mosquitos bombed Berlin, with I./NJG 1's Oberleutnant Nabrich and Hauptmann Modrow both claiming victories. Nabrich (who was flying an 'improved' He 219 that had had its armour removed and its forward-firing armament reduced to a pair of 20 mm MG 151/20 cannon) destroyed No 692 Sqn Mosquito B IV DZ608 at 0055 hrs, while Modrow brought down No 571 Sqn Mosquito B XVI MM125 at 0205 hrs. Nabrich claimed another Mosquito on 11–12 June when he destroyed No 139 Sqn B IV DZ609 at 0113 hrs.

Looking at the destruction of DZ608 in more detail, Nabrich and Habicht had been flying the 'special' He 219 throughout April and May without success, during which time they had suffered acute high-altitude air sickness, been fired on by 'friendly' Flak batteries and had a close shave with an RAF intruder.

On 10–11 June Nabrich was patrolling the Zuider Zee at 9754 m when contact was made with a fast-moving target six kilometres away flying eastwards. Even with their lightened aircraft, it took the Nabrich/Habicht team some time to close with their quarry, only attaining a good firing position when they were near Osnabrück. After a short burst from the He 219's pair of MG 151/20 cannon, the aircraft's port engine burst into flame and it began circling and losing height. When the fire reached the Mosquito's bomb-bay, it ignited the aircraft's payload with a 'gigantic flash'. Despite being blown out of the cockpit of their doomed bomber, Flg Offs Ian MacDonald (pilot) and Edward Chatfield (navigator) managed to open their parachutes and make safe landings, after which they became PoWs.

On 12 June 2./NJGr 10 lost He 219 Wk-Nr 190057 when it suffered 85 per cent damage in an accident. That same day, as a result of the ongoing battle in Normandy following the D-Day landings on the 6th, II. *Jagdkorps*' 4. *Jagdivision* issued an edict that forbade the use of SN 2 and *Neptun* radar, together with the *Naxos* and *Rosendahl* radar homers, over the Allied bridgehead. Any losses of such equipment in the area were to be reported immediately, and aircraft carrying 'special radar' were to be fitted with demolition charges. This meant that (theoretically at least) FuG 220-equipped He 219s were not allowed to operate over the coastal areas of northern France.

On the night of 12–13 June, RAF 'heavies' hit the Nordstern synthetic fuel plant in Gelsenkirchen. This raid resulted in Leutnant Hittler claiming a No 300 Sqn Lancaster B I or B III at 0130 hrs, while Hauptmann Modrow brought down no fewer than three enemy aircraft. The first of these (No 15 Sqn Lancaster B I LM156) fell at 0127 hrs, and it was followed by No 115 Sqn Lancaster B I HK545 at 0131 hrs. Modrow finished off the night with a third, unidentified, Lancaster at 0146 hrs. This last claim was confirmed by the RLM. *(text continues on page 46)*

COLOUR PLATES

1
He 219 V1 Wk-Nr 219001 VG+LW, Rostock-Marienehe, early 1943

2
He 219 V6 Wk-Nr 190006 DH+PV, *Erprobungsstelle* Rechlin, 1943

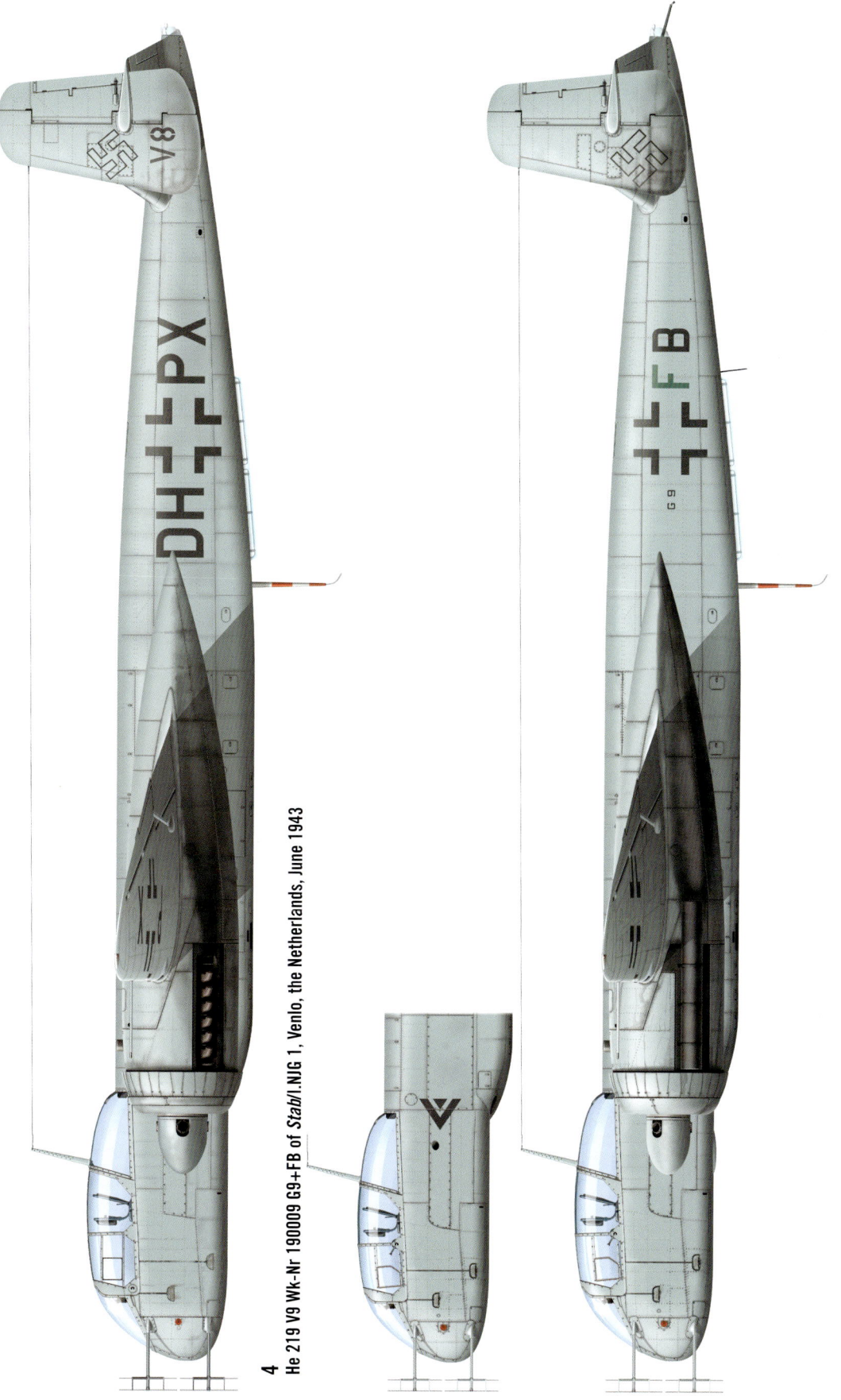

3
He 219 V8 Wk-Nr 190008 DH+PX, *Erprobungsstelle* Rechlin, September 1943

4
He 219 V9 Wk-Nr 190009 G9+FB of *Stab*/I.NJG 1, Venlo, the Netherlands, June 1943

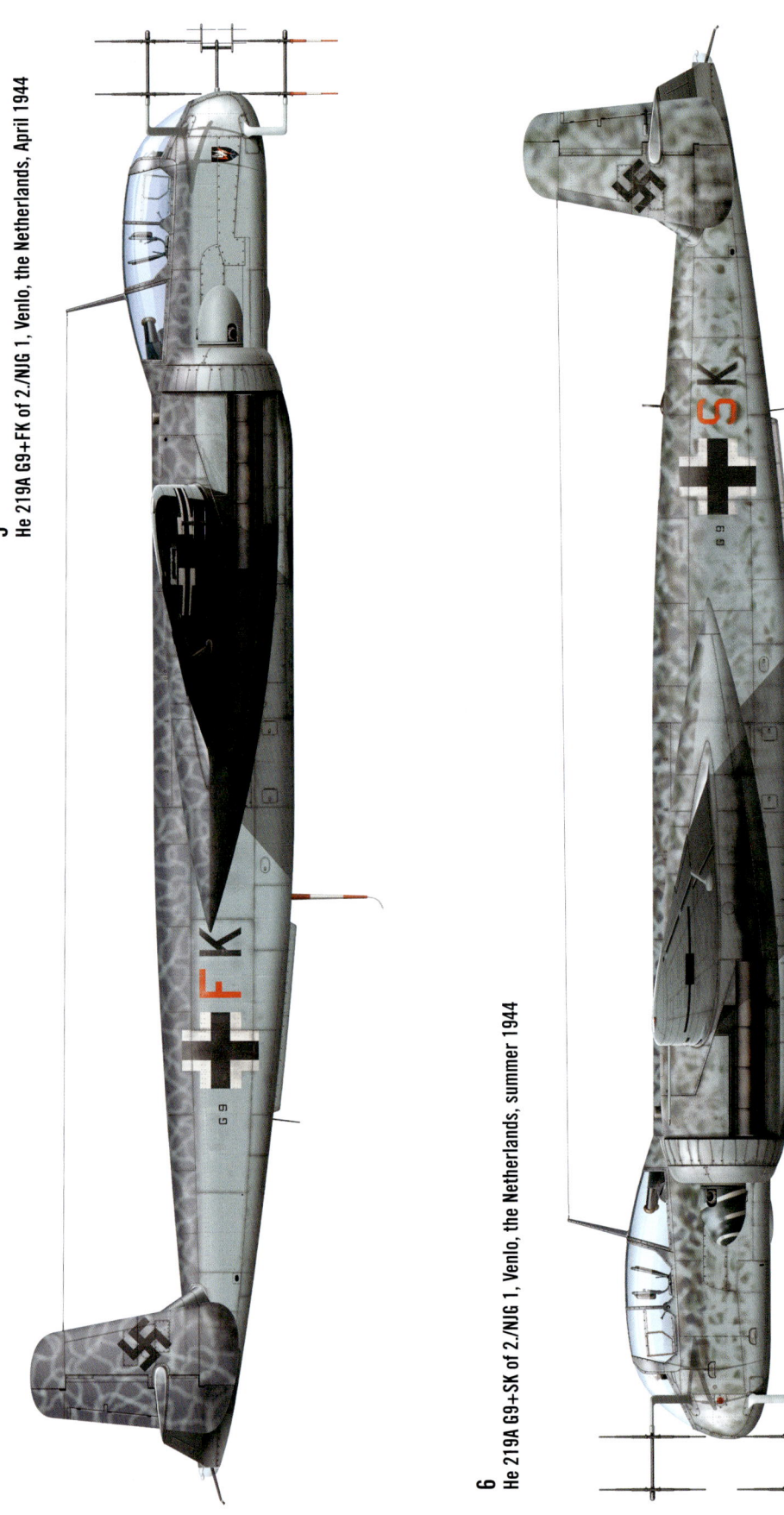

5
He 219A G9+FK of 2./NJG 1, Venlo, the Netherlands, April 1944

6
He 219A G9+SK of 2./NJG 1, Venlo, the Netherlands, summer 1944

7
He 219A-2 Wk-Nr 420331 G9+DB of *Stab* I./NJG 1, Venlo, the Netherlands, late summer 1944

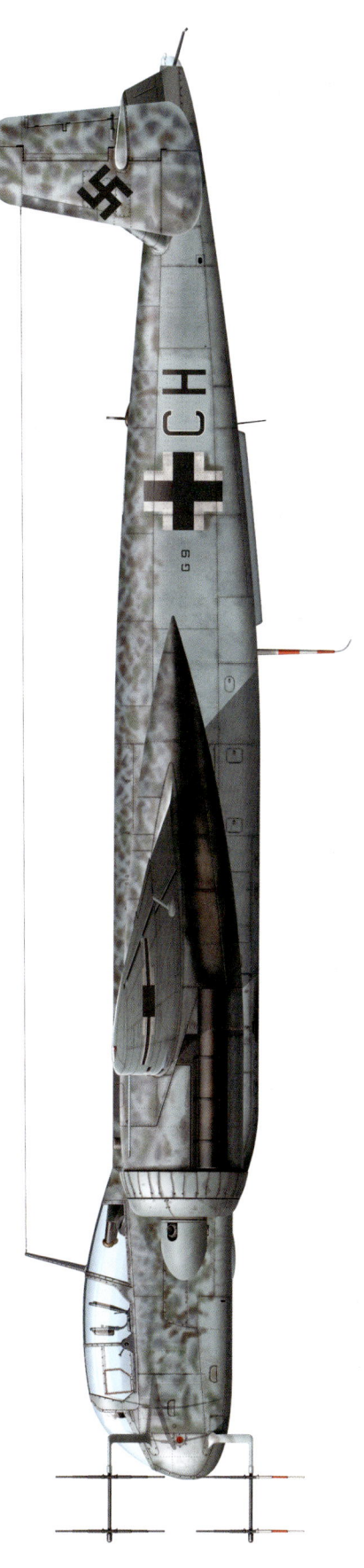

8
He 219A G9+CH of 1./NJG 1, Münster-Handorf, Germany, late 1944

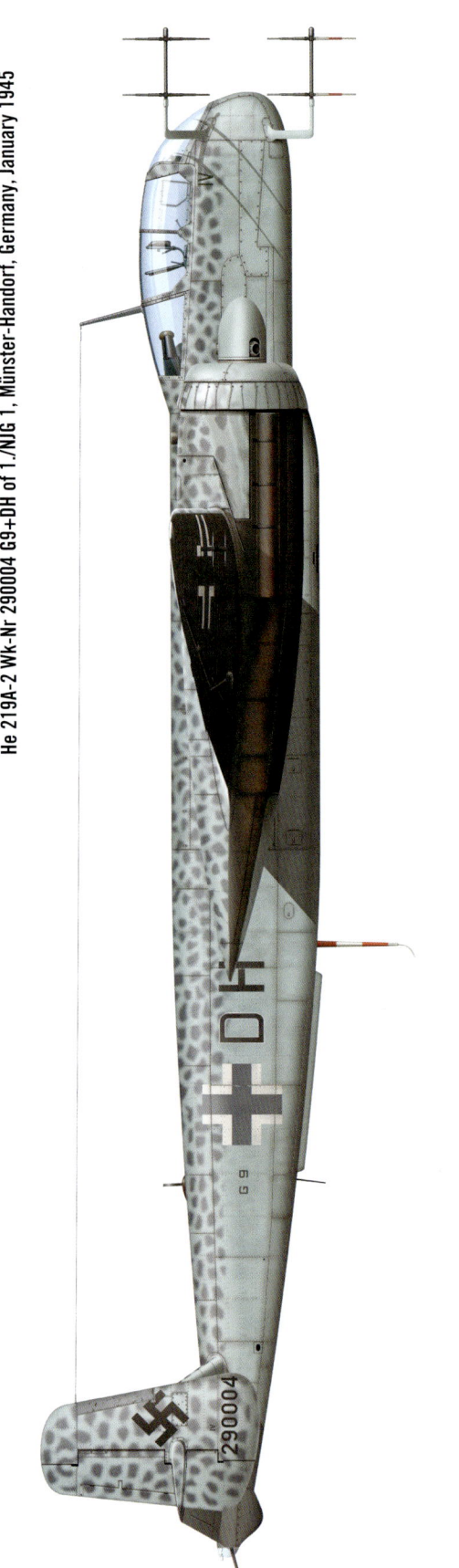

9
He 219A-2 Wk-Nr 290004 G9+DH of 1./NJG 1, Münster-Handorf, Germany, January 1945

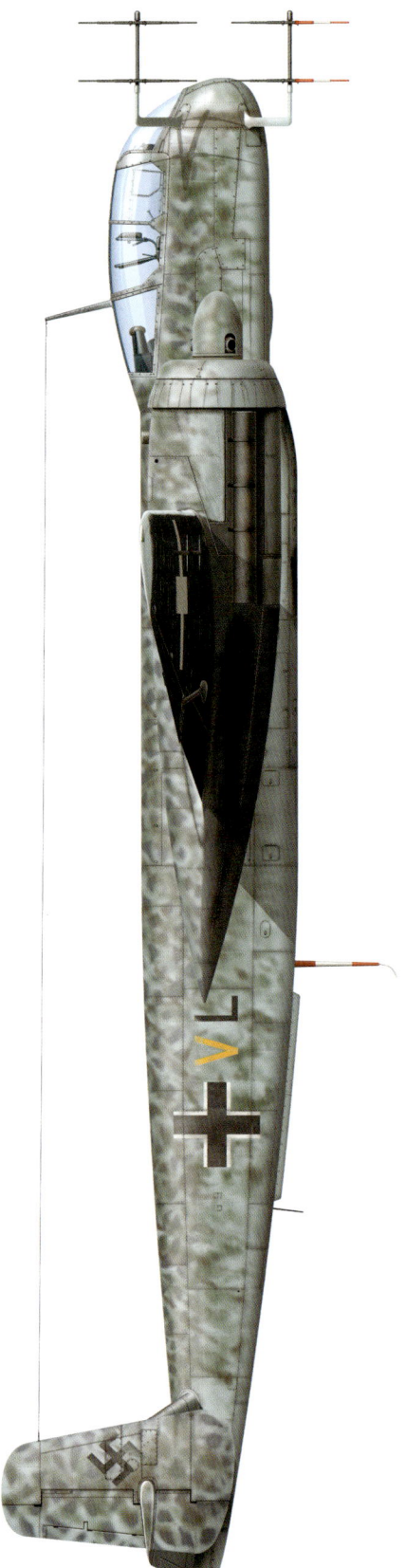

10
He 219A G9+VL of 3./NJG 1, Münster-Handorf, Germany, February 1945

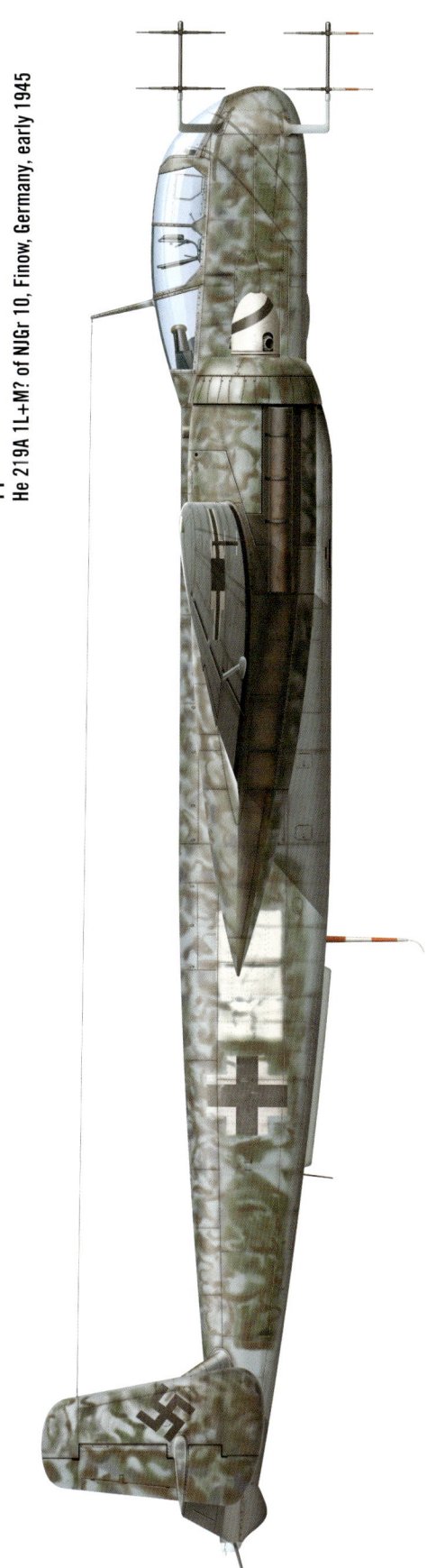

11
He 219A 1L+M? of NJGr 10, Finow, Germany, early 1945

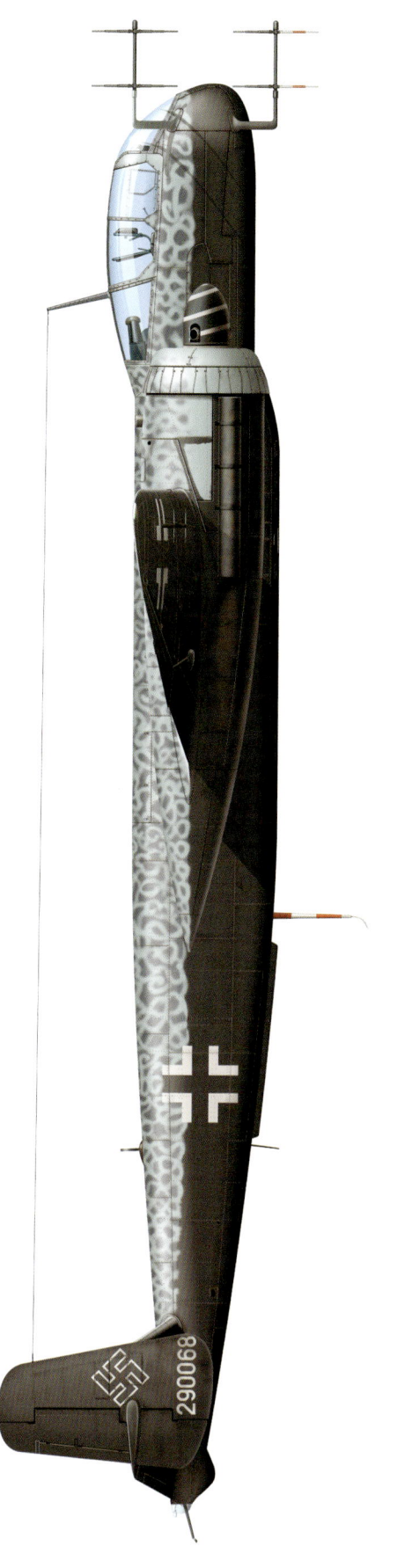

12
He 219A-2 Wk-Nr 290068, Rostock-Marienehe, Germany, autumn 1944

13
He 219A-2 Wk-Nr 290123 G9+TH of 1./NJG 1, Westerland, Germany, April 1945

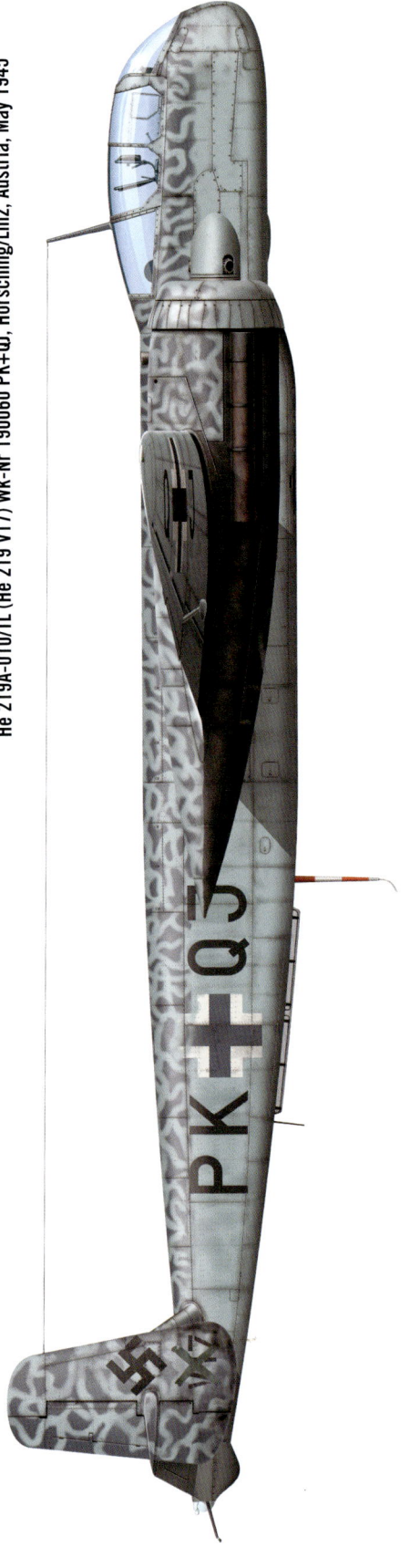

14
He 219A-010/TL (He 219 V17) Wk-Nr 190060 PK+QJ, Hörsching/Linz, Austria, May 1945

15
He 219A-065 Wk-Nr 190179 of 2./NJG 1, Westerland, Germany, May 1945

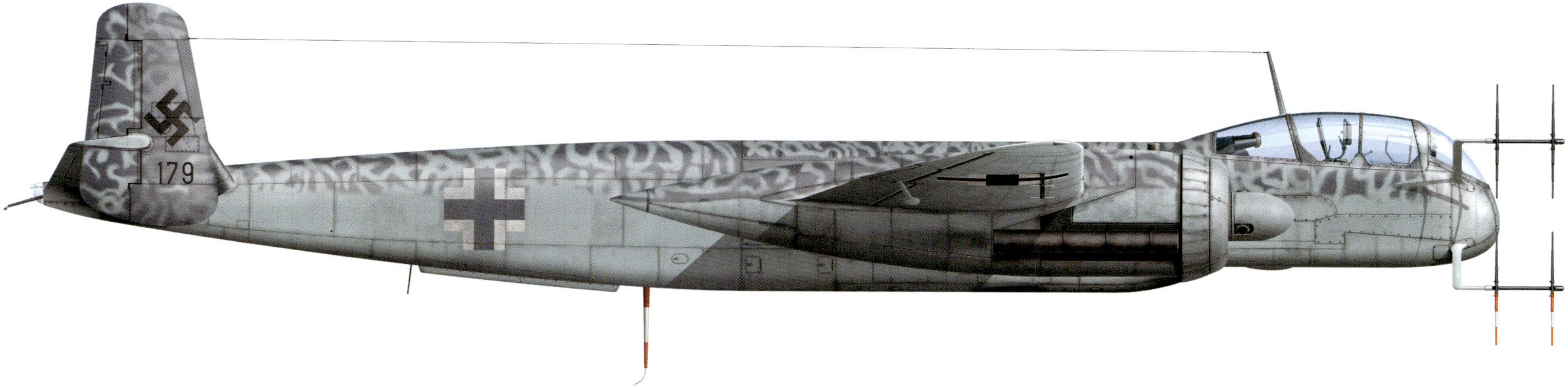

16
He 219A-7 Wk-Nr 310193 (unit and location unknown)

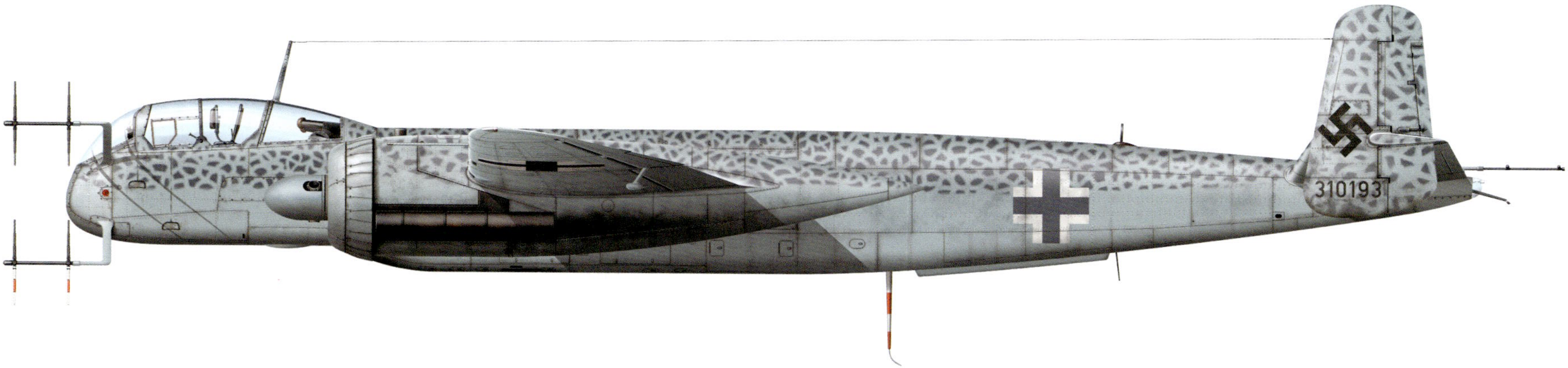

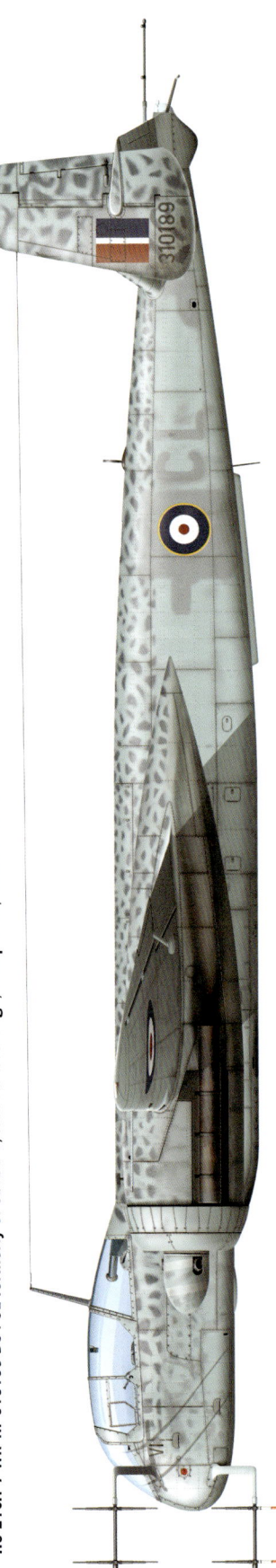

17
He 219A-7 Wk-Nr 310189 D5+CL formerly of 3./NJG 3, RAE Farnborough, Hampshire, autumn 1945

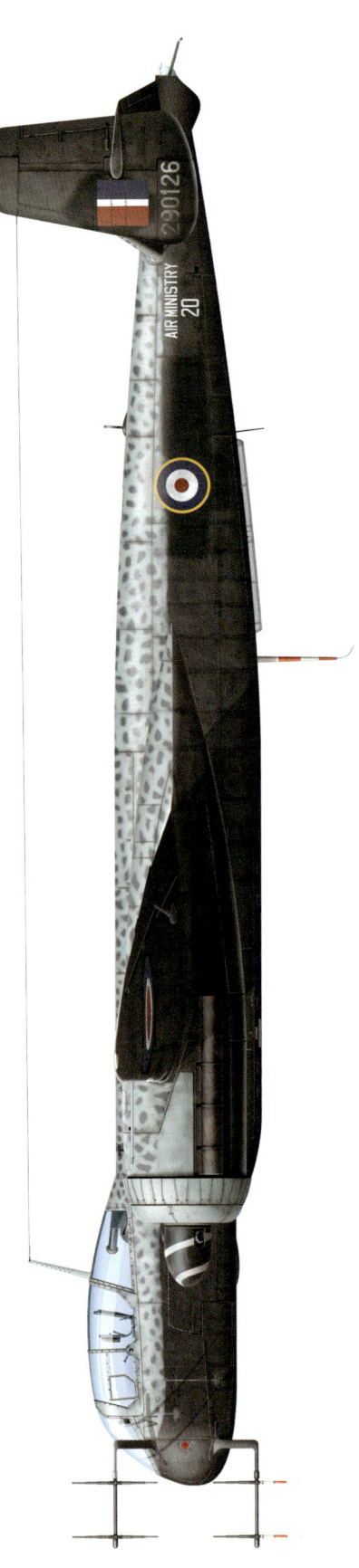

18
He 219A-2 Wk-Nr 290126 D5+BL formerly of 3./NJG 3, RAE Farnborough, Hampshire, autumn 1945

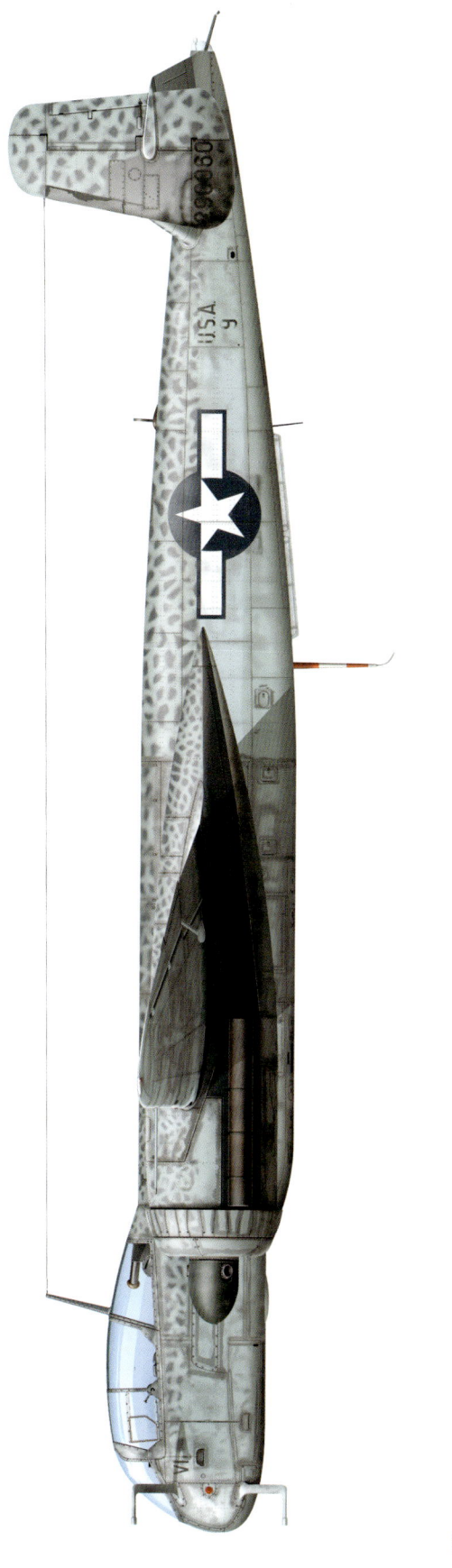
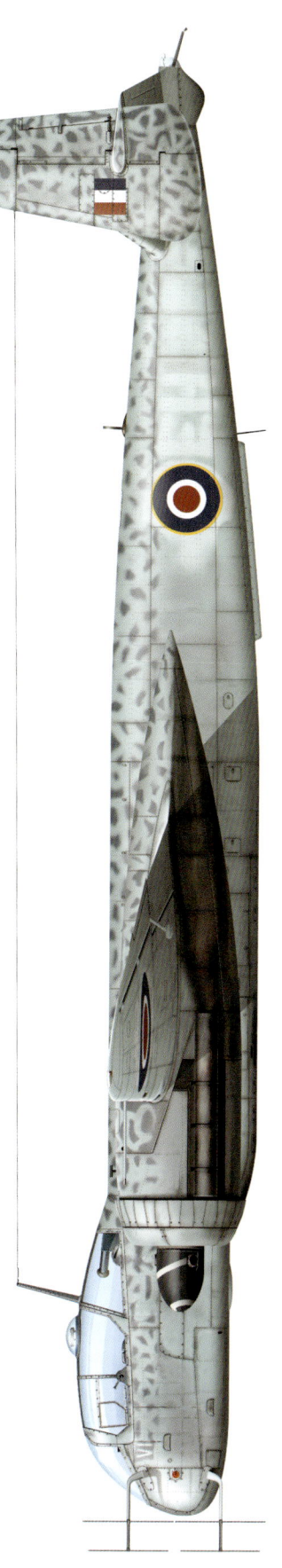

19
He 219A-2 Wk-Nr 290060, Cherbourg, France, July 1945

20
He 219A-7 Wk-Nr 310106, RAF Night Fighter Development Wing, RAF Ford, West Sussex, June 1945

Two nights later, six He 219s were scrambled to intercept another raid on Gelsenkirchen by Mosquito bombers. Among those airborne were Feldwebel Morlock (who obtained a radar contact but nothing more) and Unteroffizier Willi Beyer and his bordfunker, Obergefreiter Horst Walter. The Beyer/Walter crew (from 2./NJG 1) were in He 219A-0 Wk-Nr 190180 G9+FK, which crashed near Leersum, in the Netherlands. Beyer and Walter were killed, which was particularly ironic as both had successfully ejected from He 219 Wk-Nr 190123 on 5–6 June.

The night of 16–17 June 1944 saw the RAF 'oil campaign' continue with a strike on the Ruhrchemie synthetic oil plant at Sterkrade-Holten. A total of 14 I./NJG 1 He 219s were scrambled for *Himmelbett* GCI (four aircraft), guided *Zahme Sau* (three) and freelance *Zahme Sau* (seven) duties. Kills were claimed by 1./NJG 1's Unteroffizier Hugo Oppermann, Feldwebel Morlock, Hauptmann Strüning, Oberleutnant Baake, Oberleutnant Nabrich, Major Gert Schäfer-Suren, Hauptmann Förster and 6./NJG 1's Oberleutnant Johannes Hager.

In time order, Oppermann shot down No 434 Sqn Halifax B III LW433 at 0053 hrs, followed nine minutes later by Morlock's destruction of No 431 Sqn Halifax B III MZ520. At 0107 hrs, Strüning brought down No 550 Sqn Lancaster B I LM134, which was followed by No 77 Sqn Halifax B III MZ698, which fell to the guns of Oberleutnant Baake at 0110 hrs. Next, Nabrich downed No 431 Sqn Halifax B III NA514 at 0112 hrs, with Strüning claiming a Halifax (not confirmed by the RLM) at 0113 hrs.

The carnage continued with Morlock destroying an unidentified Halifax at 0114 hrs (the kill was confirmed by the RLM) and 6./NJG 1's Oberleutnant Hager adding No 77 Sqn Halifax B III to the growing kill list at 0120 hrs. Hager claimed a second victory (No 576 Sqn Lancaster B I ME810) at 0143 hrs. Major Schäfer-Suren weighed in at 0146 hrs when he downed No 432 Halifax B III NA516, with Nabrich claiming his second victory of the night (No 550 Sqn Lancaster B I ME840) three minutes later. Finally, Hauptmann Förster destroyed an unidentified Halifax at 0220 hrs. Again, this claim was confirmed by the RLM.

I./NJG 1 had claimed nine He 219 victories (eight confirmed and one unconfirmed), *Stab* NJG 1 one and II./NJG 1 two, bringing the night's total to 12 (11 confirmed). Interestingly, Hager's aircraft (He 219A-0 G9+LP) was one of a number of Heinkel nightfighters fitted with a ventral observation/gun position. On this occasion, it was manned by gunner/observer Feldwebel Robert Körschgen.

After a three-day respite, 21–22 June found NJG 1's He 219s opposing raids on oil targets at Wesseling, near Köln, and at Scholven-Buer. Eight He 219s were scrambled from Venlo and Deelen at 0040 hrs, and by the end of the night Hauptmann Morlock (in He 219A-0 G9+AH), Hauptmann Strüning, Oberleutnant Nabrich and Oberleutnant Baake (in He 219A-0 G9+LK) had all claimed victories.

In time order, Modrow destroyed No 9 Sqn Lancaster B I at 0112 hrs, with Hauptmann Strüning bringing down an unidentified Lancaster (confirmed by the RLM) at 0113 hrs. Three minutes later, Oberleutnant Nabrich claimed No 106 Sqn Lancaster B III LM570. At 0117 hrs, Strüning accounted for No 214 Sqn Fortress II SR381 – this radar countermeasures aircraft was, in reality, severely damaged and made it back to crash-land at RAF Woodbridge, in Suffolk. Oberleutnant Baake claimed No 49 Sqn Lancaster B I LL900 at 0122 hrs, and two minutes later Feldwebel Morlock accounted for an unidentified, but confirmed, Lancaster, with Modrow adding a second to his score when he downed another unidentified Lancaster (again confirmed by the RLM) at 0122 hrs.

At 0135 hrs, Feldwebel Morlock downed yet another unidentified, but confirmed, Lancaster, while 0139 hrs saw Strüning score his third victory of the night in the form of No 207 Sqn Lancaster B I DV360. At exactly the same time, Modrow also destroyed his third victim (No 467 Sqn Lancaster B III ED532). At 0146 hrs, Oberleutnant Baake added No 44 Sqn Lancaster B III ND552 to his growing score. Just 12 minutes later, Nabrich shot down another unidentified, but confirmed, Lancaster. At 0201 hrs Modrow destroyed his fourth bomber of the night when he downed No 50 Sqn Lancaster B I LL840. Eight minutes later, Morlock destroyed yet another unidentified, but confirmed, Lancaster, which was followed by the final He 219 kill of the night when Strüning shot down either No 44 Sqn Lancaster B III ND695 or No 630 Sqn Lancaster B III ND531 at 0230 hrs.

Strüning's victory brought the night's total to no fewer than 14 bombers destroyed by He 219s – a figure that included five sets of multiple kills. The majority of the bombers destroyed were involved in the Wesseling raid, and Morlock is described as having flown a *gefűhrte* (guided) *Zahme Sau Moskito jagd* sortie. Elsewhere, Strüning's Fortress II was I./NJG 1's 500th *Abschuss* (victory or shoot down) of the war.

Three days later, on 24–25 June, Mosquitos from RAF Bomber Command's Light Night Striking Force (LNSF) bombed Berlin, during which raid Leutnant Hittler shot down No 139 Sqn B 20 KB329 at 0137 hrs. On 27–28 June RAF 'heavies' struck at a series of rail and V1 missile targets in France. In response, I./NJG 1 and II. and IV./NJG 3 are reported to have scrambled 15 aircraft from Venlo, Plantlünne, near Lingen in Germany (II./NJG 3), and Düsseldorf (IV./NJG 3), respectively. Regarding He 219 involvement, Oberleutnant Baake (flying He 219A-0 VK G9+AK) survived a 'friendly fire' incident with a Bf 110.

The next night the LNSF attacked targets in Scholven-Buer and Saarbrücken. Oberleutnant Baake badly damaged No 109 Sqn Mosquito B XVI ML960. Flown by Flt Lt D N Russel and Flg Off J B Barker, the aircraft limped back to England, where it crash-landed at RAF Manston in Kent. Both Russel and Barker were injured in the incident, and Baake (who was flying He 219A-0 G9+AK, which was one of 12 He 219s scrambled from Venlo) fired on his quarry twice during the engagement.

In terms of inventory, 30 June 1944 is reported to have seen I./NJG 1 muster 21 He 219s, II./NJG 1 seven, *Stab* NJG 1 one and 2./NJGr 10 five. Without a doubt, June 1944 had been the He 219's most successful month to date.

July 1944 opened badly with the loss of *Stab* I./NJG 1's He 219 G9+CB on the 1st, on which date the *Gruppe* is reported to have been able to muster 21 He 219s, NJG 1's *Schulstaffel* (Training Squadron) two, 2./NJGr 10 ten and *Stab* NJG 1 and II./NJG 1 six between them.

Again, I./NJG 1 was based at Venlo, *Stab* NJG 1 and II./NJG 1 at Deelen and 2./NJGr 10 at Finow and Werneuchen, in northeastern Germany. By 7 July I./NJG 1 had 26 He 219s, 14 of which were serviceable, three were having their engines serviced, three were undergoing 'flight operations' work (usually connected with radio and/or radar equipment), three were undergoing general repair and three were having their fuselages strengthened.

In operational terms, on 1–2 July the RAF's LNSF bombed the synthetic oil plants at Scholven-Buer and Homberg. In response, I./NJG 1 scrambled six He 219s, with the aircraft flown by Oberleutnant Joachim Fincke and his bordfunker, Unteroffizier Felix Petzold, claiming No 109 Sqn Mosquito B XVI ML931 as a probable at 0138 hrs. In fact, ML931 made it back to England, where it crash-landed on one engine at RAF Woodbridge, in Suffolk. As has been alluded to before, the Mosquito was a real *bête noir* for the Luftwaffe.

Back in the combat arena, on 5–6 July Oberfeldwebel Ströhlein (in He 219 Wk-Nr 211117) destroyed 858th BS/492nd BG B-17G 4238911 at 0142 hrs. Return fire from his quarry (which crashed at Overschie, in the Netherlands) hit both of the engines in Ströhlein's He 219, and both he and his bordfunker, Unteroffizier Hans Keune, successfully ejected from their stricken aircraft.

The following night, 18 He 219s were scrambled to intercept a LNSF raid on Scholven-Buer, while 7–8 July saw RAF Bomber Command strike the V1 facility in *Saint-Leu-d'Esserent* and the railway yards at Vaires-sur-Marne, both in France, and Berlin (a Mosquito attack). I./NJG 1 scrambled 13 He 219s to engage the bombers, while NJGr 10 scrambled He 219A-0 1L+AK from Finow at 0040 hrs. This latter aircraft was flown by Major Schoenert and his bordfunker, Oberfeldwebel Johannes Richter. Elsewhere, He 219 Wk-Nr 190125 suffered 40 per cent damage in a heavy landing at Venlo.

On 9 July, I./NJG 1 had 18 serviceable He 219s, including Wk-Nr 190190 G9+PP, which had been transferred in from II./NJG 1. It had been delivered by Leutnant Fries and his bordfunker, Feldwebel Staffa, both of whom transferred to I. *Gruppe* along with their aircraft. The following night, the RAF's LNSF bombed Berlin, and of the 35 Mosquitos involved, Major Karlewski and his bordfunker, Unteroffizier Hermann Vollert (in G9+EK) claimed No 692 Sqn Mosquito B XVI PF380 shot down at 0318 hrs. By 11 July 1944, all of *Stab* and II./NJG 1's He 219s had been transferred to I./NJG 1. Another loss occurred on the 14th when Oberleutnant Joachim Fincke and his bordfunker, Unteroffizier Felix Petzold, were killed when He 219 Wk-Nr 190212 G9+LK crashed at Venlo due, it is thought, to pilot error.

The next major combat involving the He 219 came on the night of 18–19 July, when 14 aircraft were scrambled from Venlo to contest RAF raids on oil targets in the Ruhr, rail targets in France and the bombing of Berlin by 22 LNSF Mosquitos between 0025–0030 hrs. Elsewhere, the NJGr 10 Schoenert/Richter crew (in He 219A-0 1L+AK) were launched at 0020 hrs. At 0155 hrs, both I./NJG 1's Hauptmann Strüning and Unteroffizier Wittmann claimed

Seen here as an Oberleutnant upon his receipt of the Knight's Cross on 25 July 1942, Major Rudolf Schoenert was made *Kommandeur* of NJGr 10 when it was formed on 1 January 1944. A veteran of 376 combat sorties by war's end, he was credited with 62 night victories – two of these were claimed in the He 219 (*Public Domain*)

Oberfeldwebel Johannes Richter was Major Rudolf Schoenert's bordfunker for much of the war, including during his time as *Kommandeur* of NJGr 10 (*Public Domain*)

The summer of 1944 marked the high point of the He 219's service career, with examples serving with *Stab* I. and 1., 2. and 3./NJG 1. Shown here is a 1. *Staffel* example that was photographed at Westerland, on Sylt, at the end of the war (*EN Archive*)

No 571 Sqn Mosquito B XVI MM136. Almost inevitably, Strüning's claim was confirmed while the less senior Wittmann's was rejected.

On 19 July, 11 I./NJG 1 crews under Hauptmann Förster were detached to Schleswig, in northern Germany, to undertake *Himmelbett* GCI-directed *Moskito jagd* operations over north and central Germany. The detachment flew four unsuccessful missions, lost one aircraft (He 219A-0 G9+KL, which was destroyed in a failed belly landing near Schleswig on 21–22 July) and claimed a victory (No 625 Sqn Lancaster B I LM174, which was shot down by Feldwebel Morlock on 23–24 July at 0210 hrs) before returning to Venlo on the 26th.

Better fortune was had by I./NJG 1's Modrow/Schneider crew who (in G9+AH) claimed No 514 Sqn Lancaster B I HK 570 at 0157 hrs on 20–21 July during an RAF raid on the Rheinpreussen fuel plant. Three nights later, 'heavies' attacked Kiel in what was RAF Bomber Command's first area raid on a German city for two months. Venlo provided seven He 219s for the defence effort, and they were scrambled between 0021–0028 hrs. A second wave (including the Baake/Bettaque crew in He 219A-0 G9+AK) was launched by the Schleswig detachment. No victories were claimed.

On 24–25 July, I./NJG 1 launched two waves of 12 and five aircraft (60 minutes apart) to oppose an attack on Stuttgart. Again, no kills were claimed, and the night was significant as it saw the first use by the RAF of the 'long' *Window* countermeasure which was aimed at the FuG 220 AI radar that had been operating jamming-free for the previous six months.

Mixed success attended the response to the attacks on Stuttgart and Hamburg that took place on 28–29 July when I./NJG 1 scrambled 14 He 219s from Venlo between 2350–0000 hrs. Leutnant Fries, Major Shäfer-Suren and Major Karlewski all claimed to have downed enemy aircraft. Of these, Fries (in G9+DK) destroyed a Lancaster at 0115 hrs (although it was rejected by the RLM's claims commission), Shäfer-Suren another Lancaster at 0128 hrs (again, not confirmed) and Karlewski a third, confirmed, Lancaster at 0153 hrs.

The month ended with a further (albeit minor) expansion of He 219 use by the Luftwaffe. On 31 July, He 219 Wk-Nr 210901 was transferred from I./NJG 1 to the *Nachtjagstaffel* (Nightfighter Squadron, NJSt) *Finnland*, which was based at Nautsi, then in Finland (and now part of the Russian Federation). NJSt *Finnland* had initially been formed from 13(Z)./JG 5's

Nachtjagdschwarm (Nightfighter Flight) on 19 March 1944 under the command of Hauptmann Werner Hüschens, who had previously been 4./NJG 2's *Staffelkapitän*.

Wk-Nr 210901 B4+AA was the unit's only He 219, and during October 1944 it was being used by Hüschens to interdict courier aircraft flying between Leuchars, in Scotland, and Bromma, in Sweden. Other tasks included the attempted interception of RAF minelaying and SOE support aircraft operating over Scandinavia. Following the German withdrawal from Finland, NJSt *Finnland* became NJSt *Norwegen* and, finally, 4./NJG 3. In mid-January 1945, B4+AA was stationed at Lista, in southwestern Norway, and it ended the European war at Copenhagen-Kastrup, in Denmark, where it was captured by Allied forces in May 1945.

On 1 August 1944, I./NJG 1 is reported to have had a strength of 20 He 219s, with NJG 1's *Schulstaffel* assigned five and 2./NJGr 10, six. That day also saw I./NJG 1 receive He 219 Wk-Nr 210901 from the Rostock-Marienehe production line, although it lacked SN 2 radar. On the 4th, Oberleutnant Baake took off from Grove at 1000 hrs on a daylight mission against USAAF B-17 bombers that were attacking Peenemünde and Anklan, in northeastern Germany. Unbeknown to him, a groundcrewman was trapped in the rear fuselage of his He 219. Once the presence of this 'passenger' was established, Baake broke off the mission, rapidly lost height and landed at the first airfield he saw.

On 6 August, the NJGr 10 He 219s Wk-Nr 190066, 190187 and 190220 were at Werneuchen, where they were possibly being fitted with the FuG 350 *Naxos* centimetric radar homer.

Six days later, RAF 'heavies' bombed the German cities of Braunschwig and Rüsselheim. As part of the response, I./NJG 1 scrambled 14 He 219s on *ungëfuhrte* (unguided) *Zahme Sau* sorties. Of those airborne, Oberleutnant Nabrich claimed No 218 Sqn Lancaster B I PD252 at 0014 hrs, while 1./NJG 1's Unteroffizier Franz Frankenhauser destroyed No 101 Sqn Lancaster B III PB285 at 0026 hrs. Elsewhere, Hauptmann Modrow (in G9+AH) claimed a *Feindbëruhrung* (enemy contact) and a 'probable', while Leutnant Hittler (in G9+LL) was shot down by a No 169 Sqn Mosquito FB VI intruder near Wilhelmshaven, in northwestern Germany, at 0013 hrs. Both Hittler and his bordfunker, Unteroffizier Friedhelm Wildschütze, successfully ejected from their stricken fighter.

Their opponents, Flg Offs Wilfrid Miller (pilot) and Frederic Bone (navigator), had been flying FB VI NT173. Miller later recalled;

'Freddie picked up a contact crossing slightly ahead at quite a lick. We eventually caught up with it. Vertically above it, I identified it as an He 219. I dropped back to about 150 yards and gave it four two-second bursts. We were then hit by debris and lost coolant in both our engines. I glided in over the coast of Holland and Freddie bailed out at 1200 ft and I followed at 800–900 ft.'

That same day (13 August), He 219 Wk-Nr 190228 was badly damaged when its main undercarriage failed while the pilot was making an emergency landing a Stadt, near Hamburg. Shortly thereafter, Wk-Nr 190072 also belly landed at Wunstorf, near Hannover, following engine trouble. This aircraft was repairable, being returned to I./NJG 1 on 13 September 1944.

On 15 August the USAAF's Eighth Air Force and RAF Bomber Command struck at 20 Luftwaffe airfields in Belgium, northern Germany and the Netherlands. I./NJG 1's home at Venlo was hit by 104 B-17 bombers of the 390th BG, which dropped more than 1000 454 kg bombs on the airfield. Venlo was also hit by RAF Mosquitos that night, and then again on the nights of 23–24 and 28–29 August As a result of these various attacks, He 219 Wk-Nr 190175 was damaged in a landing accident on 16–17 August, as was Wk-Nr 190190 when it rolled into a bomb crater two nights later.

On the night of 15–16 August 30 LNSF Mosquitos attacked Berlin, with I./NJG 1 launching a number of He 219s against the raid at 2320 hrs. Amongst those in the air was Oberleutnant Baake (in He 219A-0 G9+AK), and despite their best efforts no victories were scored. The following night Kiel and Stettin (now Szczecin) were the targets. Two He 219s (including Wk-Nr 190213, which made a forced landing at Perleburg, near Stettin) were damaged during the action and were subsequently sent to Cheb, in the then Czechoslovakia, for repair. A third aircraft (Wk-Nr 190175) was damaged in a landing accident at Venlo.

Oil targets were to the fore on 18–19 August when the RAF bombed the synthetic oil/fuel plant at Sterkrade in the Ruhr. I./NJG 1 scrambled 14 He 219s from Venlo between 0040–0050 hrs, with Hauptmann Modrow (now I./NJG 1's *Kommandeur*, flying G9+AH) claiming a 'Lancaster' at 0209 hrs. This was actually No 51 Sqn Halifax B III LW538. During the same operation, Oberleutnant Henseler (in He 219 Wk-Nr 210904 G9+EH) suffered engine failure, and he and his unnamed bordfunker survived a subsequent belly landing at Deelen without injury – G9+EH was further damaged when it ran into a Bf 110G-4 on the ground.

The month ended with RAF Bomber Command raids on Stettin and Königsburg on the night of 29–30 August, during which Hauptmann Modrow (in G9+AH) shot down No 103 Sqn Lancaster B I LM116. Modrow went on to claim a second kill (which was never submitted for verification) before being shot down by an intruder near Grove at 0429 hrs. That same night, 2./NJG 1's Oberleutnant Baake (in G9+AK) conducted a combined *Zahme Sau/Wilde Sau* sortie over Sweden and Denmark.

1 September 1944 saw I./NJG 1 able to muster 24 He 219s, 2./NJGr 10 two and NJSt *Finnland* one. By then, Venlo had been repaired sufficiently to permit night landings, and the airfield is said to have been housing

Between July and November 1944, several He 219A-2s within the Wk-Nr blocks 290054–290078 and 290110–290129 had their undersurfaces, fuselage sides and fins and rudders finished in RLM 22. Shown here is one such aircraft, Wk-Nr 290123 G9+TH, which was photographed at Westerland in May 1945 (*EN Archive*)

a *Flöte* (flute) He 219. Allied air intelligence thought that this was 'the code name for a turbojet-assisted' aircraft. If this is correct, the *Flöte* may have been He 219A-030/He 219 V30 Wk-Nr 190101, which was built at Schwechat during late 1943 and fitted with a BMW 003 turbojet during the summer of 1944.

By 2–3 September, He 219 serviceability at Venlo had dropped to 18 aircraft, and on the 5th I./NJG 1 abandoned its long-time home and transferred to Münster-Handorf, in western Germany. Four days later, He 219s Wk-Nrs 190128 G9+OK and 210905 G9+DK were intercepted by USAAF fighters during a daylight training mission. Both aircraft were carrying three crewmen, with Unteroffizier Gustav Kramer, Obergefreiter Wilhelm Ociepka and Gefreiter Heinz Neumier aboard G9+OK and Oberfeldwebel Heinz Jadatz, Unteroffizier Alfred Schindler and Unteroffizier Heinrich Wennholz manning G9+DK. G9+OK was shot down (killing all onboard), while G9+DK made an emergency landing at Hopsten, in western Germany, and was subsequently strafed. G9+DK's pilot was killed in the incident.

Two nights later, Darmstadt and Berlin were targeted (the latter by 47 Mosquitos). I./NJG 1 scrambled eight He 219s between 2215–2230 hrs, together with the Baake/Bettaque crew (described as a 'highly experienced' *Luftbeobachter* [aerial observer] team) who took off from Münster-Handorf at 2142 hrs in He 219A-0 G9+CL. They reconnoitred the North Sea for enemy activity, while another I./NJG 1 He 219 flew a *Zahme Sau* sortie against RAF mine-layers operating over the Baltic. The following night (12–13 September), Oberleutnant Nabrich acted as the *Gruppe*'s *Aufklärer* (spotter). Taking off at 2130 hrs, he subsequently returned at 2340 hrs after having established that the 'raid' he was searching for was in fact an RAF 'Bullseye' training exercise involving aircraft that turned back before crossing the coast.

On 13 September I./NJG 1 received He 219s Wk-Nrs 190072, 190187, 211118 and 1L+EK (Wk-Nr unknown), all of which had seen service with other units. On the night of 13–14 September, 36 LNSF Mosquitos bombed Berlin and RAF Bomber Command's No 100 Group conducted a 'spoof' mission. He 219A-0 G9+CL flew a *Luftbeobachter* sortie as far as the English coast in an attempt to clarify the air picture.

By 15 September, I./NJG 1 could muster 25 He 219s (20 of which were serviceable), 32 pilots (20 of whom were combat ready) and 39 bordfunkers

An in-flight view of He 219A-2 Wk-Nr 290068, which is thought to have been photographed during a late September 1944 ferry flight to Welzow, where it was one of 34 aircraft placed in temporary storage. Points worth noting are the nightfighter's black undersides and fins and rudders and the setting of its SN 2 radar dipoles at an angle of 45 degrees to the vertical (*EN Archive*)

(22 combat ready). Unserviceable aircraft comprised Wk-Nrs 190064 (the GM-1 engine boosted He 219 V15), 190111 (ignition problems with its starboard engine), 190130 (unserviceable radio equipment), 190216 (no FuG 220 AI radar) and 190221 (transferred in from NJGr 10 at Finow).

Starting on 16 September, the period to 16 October saw I./NJG 1 have five airmen killed and two seriously injured, five He 219s (including two He 219A-2s) damaged, three (including one He 219A-2) lost in combat and one destroyed in an accident. Amongst the damaged aircraft was Wk-Nr 190216, which suffered 15 per cent damage during an RAF raid on Rheine airfield in western Germany on the night of 16–17 September.

Elsewhere, by 18 September I./NJG 1 had been reduced to 14 serviceable aircraft, two of which were fitted with the FuG 350 radar homer. On the same date, Münster-Handorf was deemed to be only serviceable for the I./NJG 1 aircraft based there following an RAF raid on the airfield on the night of 16–17 September. Reinforcements in the shape of Wk-Nrs 190229 and 190233 arrived on the 21st, with the former having no FuG 16 ZY radio fitted and the latter having no FuG 16 ZY or FuG 25 A identification friend-or-foe system installed.

I./NJG 1 was back in combat on 23–24 September when RAF Bomber Command attacked Neuss, the Dortmund-Ems Canal, Ladbergen and Münster-Handorf airfield. The *Gruppe* scrambled seven He 219s against the Neuss raid between 2134–2155 hrs, with Hauptmann Modrow (in G9+HH) claiming No 61 Sqn Lancaster B III LM718 at 2240 hrs, followed by No 78 Sqn Halifax B III MZ763 at 2311 hrs. The 'heavy raid' on Münster-Handorf resulted in Leutnant Schimer and his bordfunker, Gefreiter Rosenberger, being diverted to and crash-landing their He 219 at Ahlhorn, in northern Germany. Both survived the incident. In all probability, Schimer and Rosenberger should have been given more time to recover from the events of 23–24 September, as they were both seriously injured the following night while attempting to land at Münster-Handorf in combat-damaged He 219 Wk-Nr 190098 G9+EK.

This rather dismal month ended on the 30th when 14 USAAF B-17 bombers attacked Münster-Handorf airfield in the first of five raids that extended over the next five days. Aside from the USAAF attacks on its base on 2 and 5 October, the month opened very badly for I./NJG 1 when, on the 1st, *Gruppenkommandeur* Major Förster and his *Nachrichtenoffizier* (Intelligence Officer), Oberleutnant Fritz-Konrad Apel, were killed when their He 219 Wk-Nr 190194 G9+CL crashed while tests of blind approach provision at Münster-Handorf were being carried out. Major Förster was replaced by Hauptmann Baake on the 2nd, at which time I./NJG 1 could muster 29 He 219s, NJSt *Finnland/Norwegen* one and 2./NJGr 10 one.

On 6–7 October RAF Bomber Command struck at Köln, Dortmund and Bremen. I./NJG 1's He 219s were scrambled against the raid on Bremen, only to be recalled when it became clear that they would not be able to reach the bomber 'stream' in time. Three nights later, the RAF bombed Bochum and Wilhelmshaven, with the latter attack being executed by 47 LNSF Mosquitos. Six I./NJG 1 He 219s were scrambled at 2035 hrs, and Feldwebel Morlock claimed No 419 Sqn Lancaster B X KB754 at 2045 hrs. Elsewhere, Hauptmann Baake was airborne over the Ruhr, while Morlock identified his victim as a 'Halifax'.

On the night of 14–15 October, I./NJG 1 scrambled 14 He 219s against raids on Duisburg, Köln and Braunschweig. Unteroffizier Franz Frankenhauser and his bordfunker, Unteroffizier Helmut Biank, in Wk-Nr 190059 G9+EH were shot down by No 125 Sqn Mosquito NF XVII HK245 flown by Flg Offs G S Irving (pilot) and G Millington (radar operator/navigator).

Looking at this relatively 'run of the mill' operation in more detail gives a vivid picture of the Mosquito versus He 219 combats that were increasingly being fought out in the skies over Germany in the last months of 1944. Irving and Millington had taken off from RAF Bradwell Bay, in Essex, at 0005 hrs for a patrol over the Low Countries. Once over the Continent, the pair were put under the control of the 'Greengrocer' GCI station at Brussels-Melsbroek, in Belgium, and then under another codenamed 'Milkway'.

While flying in conditions of six-tenths patchy stratus cloud up to 1829 m, 'Milkway' alerted Irving to the presence of a 'bogey' approaching him at his '11 o'clock' position. Millington acquired the contact on his onboard AI Mk X radar and informed Irving that it was now approaching from head-on some 610 m above HK245. Turning through 180 degrees, Irving began what turned out to be a long chase at 458 km/h indicated air speed. All the while, the 'bogey' was taking violent evasive action, changing course through as much as 50 degrees while both diving and climbing.

The enemy aircraft was now heading for Duisburg (which was under attack), and fearful of losing it, Irving pushed his throttles 'through the gate' and had closed the range between the two aircraft to 914 m when two searchlights came on. The beams from these converged and then pointed eastward, signalling the 'bogey' to turn in that direction. By diving slightly, Irving narrowed the gap to 457 m, with a speed of 547 km/h 'on the clock'. Slowly, the enemy was overhauled, with HK245's crew first identifying it as a Do 217. On closer inspection, the 'Dornier' turned out to be Unteroffizier Frankenhauser's He 219.

At a range of 229 m, Irving fired a two-second burst of cannon fire that destroyed the He 219's port engine. A second burst ignited its fuselage fuel tanks, and the stricken aircraft began to dive to starboard. A third burst set the He 219's remaining engine on fire, and it entered a final spin before hitting the ground 'with a gigantic explosion'. While Frankenhauser seems to have escaped, Biank was killed. Takeaways from this skirmish include the fact that the He 219 was not an easy target to catch and the Luftwaffe's use of searchlight signalling as part of its nightfighter control system.

Biank was not the *Gruppe*'s only loss of the night, with Wk-Nr 290003 sustaining 60 per cent damage in a crash-landing at Münster-Handorf. The aircraft's pilot, Unteroffizier Werner Wollenhaupt, and his bordfunker, Unteroffizier Günther Heimesaat, were injured in the accident. During daylight on the 15th, NJSt *Norwegen* (formerly NJSt *Finnland*'s) He 219 Wk-Nr 210901 B4+AA is recorded as having been involved in a daytime convoy escort sortie together with the *Staffel*'s Bf 110s B4+IA and B4+LA. Again, B4+AA may have been flown by the unit's *Staffelkapitän*, Hauptmann Hüschens.

This rather difficult month was rounded off by an RAF raid on Wilhelmshaven on the night of 15–16 October. I./NJG 1 scrambled seven

He 219s, with the He 219A-2 Wk-Nr 290002 G9+BA or +BH being lost in what may have been a 'friendly fire' incident near Bremen. The aircraft's crew, Oberleutnant Paul-Martin Steighorst and his bordfunker, Unteroffizier Kurt Frurske, were both killed.

In something of a resurgence, I./NJG 1 claimed 18 confirmed kills and two probables during November 1944. Against this, the *Gruppe* lost both Feldwebel Morlock and 3./NJG 1's *Staffelkapitän* Oberleutnant Nabrich, together with four more crews, by month-end.

On the 1st, 2./NJGr 10 and NJSt *Norwegen* both had an He 219 apiece. The following night, Münster-Handorf scrambled 11 He 219s to oppose an RAF raid on Düsseldorf. Of these, Feldwebel Morlock and his bordfunker, Feldwebel Alfred Soika, claimed no fewer than seven confirmed victories within the 12-minute period between 1925–1937 hrs. The first of these (No 429 Sqn Halifax B III NP943) was attacked and damaged at 1925 hrs. Two minutes later, Morlock claimed a confirmed '4-motor', which was followed by a second '4-motor' at 1928 hrs. A No 49 Sqn Lancaster B III went down under Morlock's guns at 1930 hrs, with the fourth to seventh '4-motors' being brought down between 1931–1937 hrs. These seven victories were the highest number to be scored in a single mission by any He 219 crew in World War 2.

Hauptmann Werner Baake was one of I./NJG 1's more successful aces, claiming 43 night victories between June 1943 and March 1945. Awarded the Knight's Cross in late July 1944 in recognition of his growing tally, Baake was promoted to lead I. *Gruppe* three months later. He and his bordfunker, Bettaque, regularly claimed victories in the He 219 during 1944–45, and they both successfully ejected from He 219A-2 G9+AB or +BB after the aircraft was intercepted by a Mosquito XXX on 19 March 1945. Baake lost his life on 15 July 1964 when the Lufthansa Boeing 720 airliner he was flying broke up whilst attempting rolls during a training flight (*Public Domain*)

Stunning as Morlock's 'private war' might have been, he was not the only successful I./NJG 1 pilot on the night. 2./NJG 1's Unteroffizier Werner Wollenhaupt downed No 415 Sqn Halifax B III MZ603 at 1930 hrs, the bomber crashing at Rondorf on the southern edge of Köln, and 3./NJG 1's Oberleutnant Ruppert Thurner claimed No 166 Sqn Lancaster B III ND506 as a probable at 1933 hrs.

Bochum and the Dortmund-Ems Canal at Ladbergen were in the firing line on 4–5 November, with I./NJG 1 scrambling He 219s at 1813 hrs as part of the defence. At 1905 hrs, 12 of these were directed to Ladbergen, and by the end of the night Feldwebel Morlock had been killed. His aircraft (Wk-Nr 190182 G9+HL) blew up after being attacked by No 239 Sqn Mosquito FB VI PZ245. Bordfunker Feldwebel Soika managed to eject from their stricken He 219, although he was badly injured in the process.

On a more positive note, Oberleutnant Baake, 3./NJG 1's Leutnant Jürgen Prietze and 2./NJG 1's Unteroffizier Wollenhaupt had all claimed victories. For his part, Baake destroyed No 463 Sqn Lancaster B III NE133 at 1906 hrs, while Prietze brought down the first (No 426 Sqn Halifax B VI NP800) of two bombers (the second being a confirmed '4-motor') at 2004 hrs, with the second falling at 2010 hrs. Wollenhaupt's kill (No 346 Sqn Halifax B III NA546) occurred at 1830 hrs.

By 6 November, I./NJG 1 had 24 He 219s on strength, seven of which were A-2 models. That evening, RAF Bomber Command attacked Rheine, in western Germany, Gelsenkirchen, Hannover, Koblenz and the Mittelland Canal at Gravenhorst. I./NJG 1 scrambled 13 He 219s between 1900–1910 hrs, and the night's operations saw victories claimed by Hauptmann Baake, Hauptmann Modrow, Leutnant Fries and Leutnant Prietz.

In time order, Baake destroyed No 50 Sqn Lancaster B III LM628 at 1923 hrs, with Modrow (who was flying He 219A-2 G9+HH) downing No 214 Sqn Fortress III radar countermeasures aircraft HB788 three minutes later – in the heat of battle, he identified the Boeing bomber as a 'Lancaster'. Leutnant Fries (in He 219A-0 G9+GK) claimed No 106 Sqn Lancaster B I LL953 at 1927 hrs, with Modrow downing his second of the night (No 619 Sqn Lancaster B III LM742) a minute later. Fries scored his second victory when No 463 Sqn Lancaster B I NF990 went down at 1935 hrs, while 3./NJG 1's Leutnant Prietz claimed either No 463 Sqn Lancaster B I NG191 or No 207 Sqn Lancaster B III ND555 at 1937 hrs. Fries also claimed a probable, which was not filed for confirmation.

Two nights later, I./NJG 1 scrambled at least one He 219 (G9+CH), flown by Hauptmann Modrow, against a total of 19 LNSF Mosquitos. On 11–12 November the Hoesch Benzin plant at Dortmund was RAF Bomber Command's target. I./NJG 1's reaction was to despatch 13 He 219s, although none of the crews involved were able to claim a victory. A brief respite then occurred, with the RAF 'heavies' not returning until 17–18 November when Ludwigshafen was the target. 3. *Jagddivision* ordered a single He 219 *Zahme Sau* sortie that was vectored into battle via beacons *Ida* and *Otto*. Again, no claim was forthcoming.

On 21 November He 219A-2 Wk-Nr 290187 was delivered to I./NJG 1. It was the first of an influx of no fewer than 44 aircraft that were mostly sourced from existing Luftwaffe 'reserve' air parks. On the same day, three P-51 Mustang fighters of the USAAF's 339th Fighter Group were shot down by Flak at Münster-Handorf during a strafing attack, with two of the American pilots involved being killed. Sadly for I./NJG 1, another strafing incident on the 27th cost the *Gruppe* 17-victory ace Oberleutnant Nabrich, who was killed when the vehicle he was travelling in was hit on the road between Münster-Handorf and Telgte, in western Germany. Nabrich was awarded a posthumous German Cross in Gold in recognition of his combat achievements.

The end of November brought further grief when, on the 28th, No 56 Sqn Tempest V fighters caught a pair of He 219s on an early morning training flight. Wk-Nr 290019 G9+MK, flown by Leutnant Kurt Fisher and his bordfunker, Unteroffizier Hermann Bauer, was shot down in the melee, killing the pilot. The second aircraft was claimed by the RAF fighters as a probable.

Perhaps more seriously, the same day saw Heinkel being notified of problems being experienced with the wing flaps on several He 219s. By way of illustration, Wk-Nr 290009 suddenly began to roll while coming in to land and was only saved by its pilot retracting the flaps, powering up the engines and abandoning his landing. A similar situation occurred with Wk-Nr 290014, which at the time of the incident had only five hours of flying time 'on the clock'.

At the beginning of December, I./NJG 1's aircraft inventory had grown to 50 He 219s, six of which were confirmed as having been lost by year-end. Again, the *Gruppe* is logged as having received no fewer than 29 brand new Heinkel nightfighters during the course of the month – impressive numbers that in the end only resulted in one confirmed kill on the night of 24–25 December.

It is perhaps also worth bearing in mind that the month saw the He 219 shoulder a significant part of the night defence of the *Reich*, for many of the *Nachtjagd*'s other fighters were involved in flying ground support missions for Germany's final offensive in the West, which commenced in the Ardennes region of the Belgian–Luxembourg border on 16 December. This campaign was designed to deny the Allies use of the Belgium port of Antwerp as a re-supply centre, split the Allied advance and allow the encirclement of four of its armies. Despite complete surprise and some initial successes, the 'Battle of the Bulge' gradually petered out and ended in a German defeat in late January 1945. Non-use of the He 219 in the ground support role was predicated on its inability to carry bombs and the need to maintain the secrecy surrounding its crew ejection system and AI radar.

As was frequently the case in these last months of 1944, December opened badly for I./NJG 1 when, on the night of 30 November/1 December (in 'atrocious weather'), Unteroffizier Frankenhauser and his bordfunker, Gefreiter Fabian, were killed when their He 219A-2 G9+CH was shot down by an RAF intruder. The nightfighter crashed at Sendenhorst, to the southeast of Münster-Handorf.

Combat was rejoined on 2–3 December when RAF Bomber Command targeted Hagen and Giessen. I./NJG 1 sortied 20 He 219s (including the Baake/Bettaque crew aboard He 219A-2 G9+BB) between 2035–2045 hrs. Despite two 'contacts with the enemy' during the Hagen raid, no claims were made. Two nights later, a 'perceived threat to the Ruhr' drew a response from I./NJG 1. With Karlsruhe, Heilbronn/Hagen, Hamm and Bielefeld all in the frame as targets, a 'few' He 219s were scrambled. Again, no claims were made for the loss of 2./NJG 1's Oberfeldwebel Manfred Luchtmayer and his bordfunker, Unteroffizier Heinz Possett, whose He 219 (Wk-Nr 430322 G9+NK) was shot down by an intruder to the east of Münster-Handorf.

On the night of 5–6 December, Soest, Duisburg, Nürnberg and Ludwigshafen were all targeted. Once more, I./NJG 1 rose to the challenge, putting 15 He 219s into the air from Münster-Handorf at 1940 hrs. Despite 'visuals' on enemy aircraft made during the Soest raid, the intensity of the Flak over the target prevented the *Gruppe*'s He 219s from claiming any kills. To make things worse, Leutnant Fries and his bordfunker, Feldwebel Staffa, had their aircraft 'severely shot up' by an intruding No 29 Sqn Mosquito NF XIII (both crewmwen were uninjured).

However, Unteroffizier Wollenhaupt and his unnamed bordfunker, in He 219A-2 Wk-Nr 290129 G9+CK, are reported to have been killed (although this was not officially confirmed) when their aircraft crashed at Ostbevern, some eight kilometres to the east of Münster-Handorf. Other sources suggest that the Wollenhaupt crew survived the crash-landing of their aircraft at Münster-Handorf at 2205 hrs.

He 219 crews switched from being the hunters to the hunted as Mosquito NF XIIIs and XXXs appeared in increasing numbers over German skies from late 1944. Many of these aircraft, like this No 604 Sqn NF XIII photographed with its crew at B51 Lille/Vendeville, in France, in December 1944, had been moved to continental airfields from bases in England shortly after the Normandy invasion (*Public Domain*)

On 6–7 December RAF Bomber Command attacked Leuna, Merseberg, Osnabrück and Giessen – raids which drew 12 I./NJG 1 He 219s into the air against the Osnabrück force. Scrambled between 1810–1820 hrs, no claims were made. When the 'heavies' struck at Essen on 12–13 December, I./NJG 1 was grounded by the winter weather. The latter did not prevent a pair of RAF Tempest Vs destroying an He 219 on the ground at Münster-Handorf on the 17th, the aircraft veering off the airfield's runway during the attack and crashing into a nearby building. While not confirmed, the He 219 crew are thought to have survived, for no relevant loss reports have been found.

On the night of 17–18 December, Ulm, München and Duisburg were RAF Bomber Command's targets. Although scrambled, I./NJG 1 failed to make contact with any of the raiders, and Leutnant Jürgen Prietze and his bordfunker, Unteroffizier Frithjof Haake, were killed when their He 219 (G9+WL) was shot down by No 157 Sqn Mosquito NF XIX MM627 two kilometres south of Sonsbeck, on the German–Dutch border. Modern research suggests that I./NJG 1 put up aircraft in two waves at 1850–1900 hrs and at 0550–0600 hrs. At some point in the night, Oberleutnant Baake (in He 219A-0 G9+AB) was fired upon by the rear gunner of a bomber he came close to.

The following night, I./NJG 1 was airborne against raids on Gotenhafen and an RAF Bomber Command 'spoof' operation. The *Gruppe* scrambled at between 2140–2145 hrs, and was advised that the 'spoof' was a 'force of 150 heavy bombers'. No claims were made, and to make things worse, Unteroffizier Scheuerlein and his bordfunker, Unteroffizier Heinze, in He 219A-0 G9+GH were shot down by No 157 Sqn Mosquito NF XIX MM640. Both men ejected from their stricken aircraft, but Heinze was killed (when his parachute failed to open) and Scheuerlein almost strangled himself with his unplugged throat microphone lead when he ejected.

On 24–25 December I./NJG 1 finally broke its run of bad luck when the *Gruppenkommandeur* Hauptmann Baake shot down No 622 Sqn Lancaster B I NF915 at 1850 hrs during an attack on Köln. Flt Lts R J Forster and M F Newton in No 604 Sqn Mosquito NF XIII MM642 in turn claimed an He 219 as a probable, but as of this writing, the author has been unable to discover any such loss that can be matched to this claim.

Away from Münster-Handorf, Allied *Enigma*-derived intelligence put He 219s Wk-Nrs 310109 and 310113 at Parchim airfield in northern Germany on 26 December. At this time, the Allied intelligence estimate was that there were 12 Heinkel nightfighters at the base, which was believed to be the then home of NJG 1's *Schulstaffel*.

This somewhat dispiriting and frustrating month came to an end on the night of 31 December 1944/1 January 1945 when the RAF Bomber Command targeted Osterfeld, in central eastern Germany, and 3./NJG 1's *Staffelkapitän*, Oberleutnant Heinz Oloff, and his bordfunker, Feldwebel Helmut Fischer, were shot down in He 219A-2 Wk-Nr 290194 G9+KL. They fell victim to No 169 Sqn's Sqn Ldr 'Dickie' Drew (radar operator/navigator) and Flt Lt Paul Mellows (pilot) flying borrowed No 85 Sqn Mosquito NF XXX MT491. Mellows' account of this combat reads as follows;

'We had obtained a contact at six miles range and chased [it] slowly to port and climbed from 15,000 ft to 18,000 ft. While the contact was still well above, another came in at three miles range from the west nearly head on. This was found to be at our height, so we turned to starboard as it passed us and came in 4000 ft behind. A visual was obtained at 2000 ft on four white exhausts, and on closing to 400 ft, twin tail fins were seen, and shortly after, black crosses on the blue undersurfaces of the wings, which were seen in the light of a searchlight.

'On the strength of this I fired a two-second burst from slightly below, causing debris to fly off and starting a small fire in the fuselage. Another two-second burst caused an explosion, by the light of which Dickie [Sqn Ldr Drew] clearly saw the dihedral and slanting fins of an He 219, which I confirmed. A further short burst set him alight, and from 1000 ft to starboard we saw him climb for a few seconds before plunging to earth, where he exploded with a bright orange flash at 1824 hrs. Throughout the combat the He 219 was flying straight and level, and appeared to have no knowledge of our presence.'

The I./NJG 1 aircraft sortied that night had scrambled from Münster-Handorf at 1740 hrs, and alongside the Oloff/Fischer crew (who successfully ejected from their damaged aircraft and returned to combat duties the following February), the Baake/Bettaque crew (in He 219A-2 G9+AB) and 3./NJG 1's Feldwebel Hans Sieben were airborne. For his part, Sieben stated that he had downed a Lancaster, but the claim was not confirmed.

CHAPTER FOUR

ENDGAME

By the end of January 1945, I./NJG 1 had received no fewer than 73 He 219s – a largesse that facilitated the creation of a new unit equipped with the aircraft that had been first conceived during the previous October. Accordingly, the month saw preparations begin for the conversion of I./NJG 3 to the type, with activity taking place at Parchim, Ludwigslust and Grove airfields in northeast Germany and Denmark. In the event, the conversion proceeded at a snail's pace, and while definitely receiving He 219s, I./NJG 3 appears to have continued flying *Einsatz* (operational) missions using Ju 88 fighters until the end of the war in Europe in May 1945.

Returning to I./NJG 1, the *Gruppe* reported a strength of 66 He 219s on 1 January 1945 (with NJSt *Norwegen* declaring just one). The unit's first operational scramble of the month came on the night of 1–2 January when I./NJG 1 formed part of the defensive response to the RAF's bombing of Vohwinkel and the Mittelland Canal at Gravenhorst. Airborne between 1800–1925 hrs, the *Gruppe*'s war diary records that 'many visual contacts' were made but none resulted in combat due to the FuG 220 AI radar jamming being 'so strong' as to render the 'holding of targets' impossible. The following night, the RAF struck at Ludwigshafen, Nürnberg and Berlin, with the attack on the German capital being made by 53 LNSF Mosquitos. I./NJG 1 was unable to intervene due to dense fog preventing flying from its base at Münster-Handorf.

In the final weeks of the war in Europe, many He 219s were blown up by their German owners to prevent them from falling into Allied hands. Shown here is one such wreck that had formerly been 1./NJG 1's He 219A-2 Wk-Nr 290004 G9+DH. One of the identification features that marked out He 219A-0, A-2, A-7 and D-1 aircraft was their use of enlarged fins and rudders (as seen here) when compared with those fitted to the He 219 V1. Note the suppressed FuG 16 radio antenna built into the assembly's upper leading edge (*EN Archive*)

Moving back to NJG 3, on 3 January Allied intelligence registered the presence of two He 219s and four Ta 154s at Stade, in northern Germany. As the Ta 154 was believed to have been assigned to III./NJG 3, the presumption was that all these aircraft were from that *Geschwader*. On firmer ground was the interception by *Enigma* of a 5 January request for technical staff (including some from Heinkel), technical data and demonstration material to be sent to Grove to assist in I./NJG 3's conversion to the He 219.

On the combat front, 5–6 January 1945 saw the RAF bomb Hannover, Hooffalize and Berlin (with the latter attack again being carried out by two waves of LNSF Mosquitos), together with a 'spoof' raid against Heligoland. Like the Berlin strikes, the attack on Hannover was a double raid. I./NJG 1's Leutnant Fries (assigned to 2./NJG 1 and flying G9+EK), Hauptmann Baake (*Stab* I./NJG 1) and Hauptmann Modrow (1./NJG 1) all claimed kills.

In time order, Fries began the night's events when he destroyed No 635 Sqn Lancaster B III PB564, which had been participating in the 'spoof', at 1905 hrs. At exactly the same time, Hauptmann Baake claimed another 'spoofer' in the form of a No 100 Group Halifax, followed by a second No 100 Group Halifax at 1912 hrs. At 1944 hrs, Baake downed his third victim of the night when he destroyed No 425 Sqn Halifax B III MZ860, which crashed 50 km west of Hannover. Finally, the Modrow/Schneider crew (in He 219A-0 G9+HH, which was airborne between 1811–2037 hrs) claimed a confirmed, but unidentified, Halifax – a kill that was to be Modrow's last of the war.

As was becoming increasingly common, victories now came at some cost to the He 219 crews. On 5–6 January, I./NJG 1's Oberfeldwebel Josef Ströhlein and Oberfeldwebel Hans Keilich were brought down by the enemy. Having set a Lancaster on fire, which was claimed as a probable, Ströhlein (in He 219A-0 Wk-Nr 190186 G9+CK) was shot down by No 157 Sqn Mosquito NF XIX TA394. Although Ströhlein was killed in the incident, his bordfunker, Unteroffizier Hans Keune ejected successfully. G9+CK crashed five kilometres south of Wesendorf in central-north Germany. In Keilich's case, he and his unnamed bordfunker were attacked by a Mosquito intruder that set G9+BH's starboard engine on fire. The crew ejected successfully, with Keilich being injured in the incident.

In a final act of mayhem, 1./NJG 1's Oberleutnant Henseler and his bordfunker, Leutnant Kienle, had just landed in Wk-Nr 190226 at Grove when the aircraft was shot up by No 406 Sqn Mosquito NF XXX NT283 as it taxied into the dispersal area. The Heinkel was repaired, only to then be written off when it suffered 80 per cent damage in another incident in April.

Losses continued for I./NJG 1 on 7 January when Unteroffizier Karl Barkenfeld and his bordfunker, Obergefreiter Ernst Frendenberger, were killed when their aircraft (Wk-Nr 290072) crashed at Bad Iburg, in northwest Germany. In this instance, no enemy action was involved. Three days later, I./NJG 1 reported that 45 of its 64 He 219s were serviceable, while at I./NJG 3, 12–13 January saw Unteroffizier Harling and Leutnant Werner Golze undertake *Umschulungsflüge* (retraining or conversion flights) in He 219s.

I./NJG 1 was called into action again when the RAF bombed Saarbrücken and Politz on the night of 13–14 January. I./NJG 1 aircraft were scrambled without success, and on the same night, NJSt *Norwegen*'s He 219 B4+AA was operational from Lista, in Norway, with, it is thought, the intent of intercepting a courier aircraft flying between Scotland and Sweden.

Returning to Germany, on 14 January 3./NJG 1's Leutnant Reinhard Lehr (in Wk-Nr 290125 G9+PL) was attacked and shot down near Münster-Handorf during a daylight training sortie. Lehr was caught by No 274 Sqn Tempest V EL762. That same day, further to the east, Leutnant Mausz and his six-man detachment arrived at Ludwigslust to undertake the 'conversion' of a number of He 219s. Whilst not spelt out, this was probably connected with the installation of *Schräge Musik* weaponry into the Heinkel nightfighter, which (according to Allied *Enigma*-derived intelligence) involved a programme of 18 aircraft.

I./NJG 1's next clash with the RAF came on the night of 14–15 January when the synthetic fuel plant at Leuna was bombed. As was becoming disturbingly familiar, the *Gruppe* was scrambled (including the Fries/Staffa crew in G9+EK) without success.

Two nights later, fuel and oil were again on the RAF's target list, with attacks being made on Magdeburg and the synthetic fuel plants at Zeitz (near Leipzig), Wann-Eickel (in the Ruhr) and at Brüx (in what was then Czechoslovakia). I./NJG 1 scrambled five He 219s flown by *Spitzenbesatzungen* (first class) crews, with 3./NJG 1's Feldwebel Hans Sieben claiming an unidentified Lancaster from the Zeitz raid. Better results were thwarted by the failure of the 'reportage' (the broadcast running commentary that directed the *Zahme Sau* nightfighters into the bomber 'streams'). On the downside, the Fries/Staffa crew (in He 219A-2 G9+EK) were shot down by a marauding No 85 Sqn Mosquito NF XXX. Both Fries and Staffa ejected and landed safely.

On 17 January, 3./NJG 3's Hauptmann Eduard Schröder made a 15-minute *Platflug* (local flight) in an He 219, and eight days later 3. *Jagddivision* (which included I./NJG 1) advised its units that all 'SN 2 [AI radar] spot frequencies [and] *Naxos-Z* and *Flensburg* [homing equipments]'

Despite (or perhaps because of) apparently never having used the He 219 in combat, a number of NJG 3 aircraft were captured in airworthy condition at Grove in May 1945. Shown here is He 219A-7 Wk-Nr 310189 DB+CL, which was brought to Britain for testing, where it was given the Air Ministry number 22 (*EN Archive*)

were released for 'nightfighting over enemy and neutral territory', thereby lifting restrictions which had been in place since the previous October. Whether this applied to the He 219 (due to the continuing secrecy concerning its crew ejection system) was not made clear.

The month ended with He 219A-2 Wk-Nr 420320 suffering 25 per cent damage at Ludwigslust on 27 January.

On 1–2 February Feldwebel Günther Thurow and his bordfunker, Unteroffizier Neff, flew an interesting three-hour, *Orgelpfeife* (organ pipe) sortie in He 219 G9+WH. *Orgelpfeife* was the codename used to describe operations that generated 'spoof' nightfighter radio communications traffic to give the impression of activity on a larger scale than was the reality. Knowing that the 'enemy was listening', it was hoped that *Orgelpfeife* would mis-direct any real-time responses to the apparent ongoing air picture. Elsewhere, 1–2 February saw the Modrow/Staffa crew shot down by No 25 Sqn Mosquito NF XXX MV521 near Köln. The He 219 crashed at Hennef, in west Germany, and both Modrow and Staffa made successful ejections. Incredibly, this was Staffa's third such ejection from an He 219!

Alongside Modrow, another pilot in trouble that night was Unteroffizier Hugo Oppermann, who was flying He 219A-2 Wk-Nr 290004 G9+DH. Whilst attempting an emergency landing at Paderborn, he hit an obstacle upon touching down. The ensuing crash resulted in 290004 incurring 40 per cent damage. It is not confirmed whether the aircraft's crew survived the incident. The night appears to have been rounded off by Hauptmann Baake performing (according to bordfunker Bettaque) a 'criminal landing' following radio failure aboard their He 219.

RAF Bomber Command's growing air superiority is well illustrated by its operation on 1–2 February when it struck at no fewer than nine targets, with bombs falling on Ludwigshafen, Mainz, Siegen, Bruckhausen (LNSF), Mannheim (LNSF), Stuttgart (LNSF), Nürnberg (LNSF), Hannover (LNSF) and Berlin (LNSF). Of these, the LNSF operations involved some 74 Mosquito sorties.

Oil targets predominated on 3–4 February, when the synthetic fuel plants at Bottrop and Dortmund were targeted. I./NJG 1 scrambled five He 219s to oppose these, with Hauptmann Baake and the grandly named Hauptmann Alexander Graf Rosséguier de Miremont making claims.

In the order given, Baake claimed an unidentified (but RLM confirmed) Lancaster from the Dortmund raid at 2007 hrs, followed by a probable (another Lancaster). Rosséguier (in 1./NJG 1's Wk-Nr 290070 G9+OH) downed an unidentified (but confirmed) Lancaster from the Dortmund 'stream' at approximately 2030 hrs. This 'heavy' came down near Roermond, in the Netherlands. Unfortunately for Rosséguier, his victim fought back, the bomber's rear gunner wounding him in the face and seriously damaging his aircraft. He and his bordfunker, Feldwebel Fritz 'Pitt' Habicht, duly ejected, with the latter suffering a spinal dislocation that saw him hospitalised. Prior to flying the He 219, Rosséguier had served with NJG 5 following a spell as *Gruppenkommandeur* of II./JG 301 in August–November 1943.

That same night (3–4 February 1945), I./NJG 1's Feldwebel Günther Thurow and his bordfunker, Unteroffizier Neff, survived a single-engined crash-landing at Münster-Handorf following an attack on their aircraft (Wk-Nr 290058 G9+VH) by No 414 Sqn Mosquito NF XXX NT281 that was being flown by Flt Lts B N Plumber (pilot) and E H Collis (radar operator/navigator).

The Thurow/Neff shoot down is a good illustration of the conditions in which the He 219 crews were operating at this late point in the European war. Plumber and Collis had taken off on patrol from Amiens-Glisy, in northern France, while Thurow and Neff were ordered to orbit the radio beacon *Gemse* (Chamois) that was situated between Krefeld and Mönchengladbach.

After 15 minutes circling the beacon at an altitude of some 7925 m, Thurow got the shock of his life (the more so because he had been studiously carrying out the standard 'anti-Mosquito' procedure of constantly varying his aircraft's attitude and speed) when Plumber pounced. Immediately, he broke to port and dived for the ground. Plumber followed him down, but when his aircraft reached a speed of 724 km/h at 5182 m he levelled off for fear of overstraining his Mosquito. Taking advantage of the He 219's superior diving capabilities, Thurow succeeded in throwing off his attacker. Having then managed to extinguish the engine fire that the initial attack had started, he made for Münster-Handorf on his remaining good engine.

On approaching the airfield, Thurow discovered that his flaps and undercarriage were inoperable. Despite use of the damaged aircraft's back-up compressed air system, his undercarriage still refused to function and he was left with no option other than to attempt a belly landing. Having survived this, Thurow and Neff were able to climb out of their battered (but ultimately repairable) aircraft, just in time to see another He 219 make a crash-landing and burst into flames! This second aircraft may have been Wk-Nr 190235, and as of this writing, the author has been unable to uncover whether or not its crew survived.

Activity continued at Ludwigslust, with the arrival of the Rostock-Marienehe-built He 219A-7s Wk-Nrs 310203, 310208 and 310209 during the period 4–7 February. It is assumed that these aircraft were delivered for the installation of their *Schräge Musik* oblique-firing weapons. On the 6th He 219A-2 Wk-Nr 420324 suffered 20 per cent damage in a hard landing that was attributed to pilot error.

The following night (7–8 February), the RAF attacked another clutch of 11 targets that included Kleve, Goch and Dortmund and LNSF raids on eight separate locations. In response, NJG 1 scrambled seven *Spitzenbesatzungen*-crewed He 219s from Münster-Handorf at 2100 hrs. This practice of dividing a unit's crews into competence categories and only launching the most experienced was becoming increasingly common within the *Nachtjagd*. This was primarily because dwindling fuel supplies limited the number of aircraft that could be sortied against any particular raid, and any level of effectiveness (or, indeed, survival) required flyers with the most operational experience.

Unfortunately, on this night, it did not work, with the *Gruppe*'s war diary noting that none of its crews were able to infiltrate the bomber 'stream' as it was 'too far away'. To add to the misery, 3./NJG 1's Oberfeldwebel Hans Sieben and his bordfunker, Unteroffizier Walter Stiefellhagen, had to eject at 800 m near Münster-Handorf when one of the engines of their He 219A-2 (Wk-Nr 290203) caught fire following combat damage inflicted by 'friendly' flak. The aircraft crashed near Telgte, in northwestern Germany. Despite what was considered to be a low-altitude ejection from an He 219, both Sieben and Stiefellhagen survived.

By this point in the war, it was not only the *Nachtjagd*'s aircraft that were suffering but also the Luftwaffe infrastructure. For example, on 12 February Münster-Handorf declared that it was only serviceable for 'its own aircraft', while Ludwigslust's soft surface was deemed useable 'in an emergency' only. For its part, the airfield at Grove was marked as being 'conditionally serviceable' (but unserviceable in bad weather) due to construction work being undertaken on the runway.

I./NJG 1 was not involved in the controversial twin raid on Dresden in eastern Germany that took place on 13–14 February and which produced a 'fire storm' that killed as many as 25,000 people. The following night, Chemnitz, Rositz, Duisburg (LNSF) and Mainz (LNSF) were 'blitzed'. This time, I./NJG 1 was scrambled twice, with a first wave of four He 219s taking off between 1930–1959 hrs to contest the Chemnitz attack, and a second (again, of four aircraft) subsequently launching against the Rositz raid.

In the first instance, the *Gruppe*'s war diary reports that 'some of the aircraft [were] correctly sluiced into the bomber stream' but could not remain within it due to an 'inadequate running commentary' failing to provide enough direction for contact to be maintained. Again, the *Gruppe* suffered another loss to an intruder when the unfortunate Sieben/Stiefellhagen crew (perhaps 'back in the saddle' too early following their adventures of 7–8 February) were shot down by No 406 Sqn Mosquito NF XXX NT325 near Nordhausen (the site of the infamous underground 'Dora' aircraft and missile factory staffed largely by concentration camp inmates and other forced labourers who died in large numbers) in central Germany at 2230 hrs. Once again, both crewmen ejected from their stricken aircraft (Wk-Nr 310213), with Stiefellhagen suffering from burns and other injuries sustained during the incident.

For his part, Modrow (who was airborne in G9+CH) is understood to have achieved three contacts with enemy aircraft, all of which failed due to the inadequacy of the 'close range resolution of his onboard radar'. Whether this indicated that G9+CH was equipped with an early-model FuG 220 with poor close-up resolution or that his SN 2 radar had simply failed is not made clear.

On 20–21 February, the RAF bombed three targets in the Ruhr together with the Mittelland Canal at Gravenhorst. On this occasion, I./NJG 1 was grounded by a 100 m cloud base over Münster-Handorf.

The following night, Gravenhorst, Duisburg and Berlin (two waves of LNSF Mosquitos) were struck. Seven He 219s were scrambled on *Verfolgungsnachtjagd* (pursuit nightfighter) sorties between 1932–2010 hrs, with Hauptmann Schirrmacher (assigned to 1./NJG 1) claiming an unidentified '4-motor' south of Duisburg. His aircraft (He 219A-0 G9+TH) was hit by return fire, wounding Schirrmacher in the foot, head and face. With the ejector seats aboard his nightfighter inoperable, he and his bordfunker, Feldwebel Waldmann, made a successful emergency landing at Dortmund with 30 per cent battle damage to their aircraft.

At 2236 hrs I./NJG 1 launched a second wave of six He 219s, none of which (despite one aircraft obtaining two visual contacts) were able to make any claims. Elsewhere, the *Gruppe*'s Oberleutnant Henseler suffered engine failure during his patrol.

Another dismal month was rounded off on 23–24 February when the RAF hit Pforzheim, in Germany, and Horten, in Norway, as well as dropping sea mines off the Norwegian coast. I./NJG 1's war diary recorded that there were 'no orders for take-off, only cockpit readiness'. The next night, I./NJG 1 may or may not have been sent up against an RAF Bomber Command 'spoof' raid that was directed towards Düsseldorf. Any He 219s that did participate failed to bring down any of the five Halifax bombers that the RAF lost during the operation.

In terms of combat performance, March 1945 was little better for I./NJG 1 than the preceding one had been. During the month, the *Gruppe* was only able to claim the destruction of two Lancasters for the loss of three He 219s and the injuring of two of their crew. Again, the maximum number of I./NJG 1 aircraft scrambled on any one night was six, while I./NJG 3 still showed no signs of completing its conversion to the He 219. Indeed (and as noted elsewhere), the *Gruppe*'s operations through to April 1945 all appear to have been flown by Ju 88 nightfighters.

With regard to the He 219, combat was resumed on 3–4 March when the RAF bombed, amongst other places, the synthetic fuel plant at Berkamon, the Dortmund-Ems Canal, Berlin (LNSF) and Würzburg (LNSF), together with 'Gardening' in the Kattegat and off Oslo. I./NJG 1 scrambled five He 219s, including those flown by the Baake/Bettaque (G9+AB) and Oloff/Fischer (He 219 V41 G9+BL) crews on *Zahme Sau Verfelgungsnachtjagd* (pursuit nightfighting) sorties.

The most interesting of the *Gruppe*'s aircraft that were operational that night was G9+BL, which was He 219A-2 airframe Wk-Nr 420325 that had been fitted with Jumo 213E engines with MW 50 power boost in place of the type's standard DB 603 motors. Back in July 1944, Heinkel's technical director had estimated that a Jumo 213E-powered, fully equipped (with radar aerials and engine flame dampers installed) He 219 would have a maximum speed of 605 km/h at 10,500 m, rising to 635 km/h at 9500 m with the addition of MW 50. By way of comparison, a fully equipped DB 603-powered aircraft could achieve a top speed of 585 km/h at 7500 m. The V41 began operational trials with 3./NJG 1 on 21–22 February.

Baake/Bettaque (G9+AB) and Oloff/Fischer (G9+BL) were scrambled again on the night of 5–6 March when RAF Bomber Command attacked the Braunkohle-Benzin synthetic fuel plant at Böhlen. As was becoming depressingly familiar, there were no victory claims. 6–7 March told a similar story, with I./NJG 1 scrambling three He 219s (including G9+EK, which was flown by the Fries/Staffa crew) against a raid on Wesel. Again, there were no claims.

Two nights later, the RAF struck at the Deutsche Erdöl refinery at Hemmingstedt, in northern Germany, Harburg, Dessau, Berlin (LNSF), Frankfurt (LNSF), Münster (LNSF) and Hannover (LNSF). To add insult to injury, a force of USAAF B-24s bombed Dortmund in support of an RAF No 100 Group 'spoof' operation. I./NJG 1 scrambled six He 219s against the Dessau raid, with Hauptmann Baake and 3./NJG 1's

Oberleutnant Ruppert Thurner claiming kills. For his part, Baake destroyed a Lancaster south-southeast of Dortmund at 2017 hrs, while Thurner downed an unidentified '4-motor' near Magdeburg. These two kills were I./NJG 1's only victories during March 1945.

I./NJG 1's He 219s were back in action on 18–19 March when Witten, Hanau, Berlin (LNSF) and Nürnberg (LNSF) were bombed. Six He 219s were scrambled against the Hanau raid, including the Fries/Staffa crew (in G9+EK), Modrow (in G9+HH), Oloff/Fischer (G9+BL), Sieben and the Baake/Bettaque crew (in He 219A-2 G9+AB or +BB). Of these, Fries and his bordfunker, Feldwebel Staffa 'returned early' when their onboard intercommunication system failed, as did Modrow when his aircraft's starboard engine began to run roughly. At 0520 hrs, No 219 Sqn Mosquito NF XXX NT271 caught and shot down Baake's aircraft, which crashed between Olpe and Kreuztal near Siegen, in west central Germany. Baake and Bettaque ejected safely and emerged from the incident uninjured.

In a foretaste of things to come, five He 219s were damaged in a strafing attack on Münster-Handorf by USAAF P-47 fighter-bombers on the 20th. That night, RAF Bomber Command hit Böhlen, Hemmingstedt and Kassel (LNSF), with I./NJG 1 scrambling five He 219s against the latter force. Amongst those airborne were 3./NJG 1's Oloff/Fischer and Fries/Staffa (in G9+EK) crews.

Oloff and Fischer were shot down by No 85 Sqn Mosquito NF XXX NT324 flown by Flt Lt G Chapman (pilot) and Flt Sgt J Stockley (radar operator/navigator). Oloff/Fischer were flying the Jumo 213E-powered He 219 V41, which had undergone less than a full month's evaluation and whose loss was deemed to have been a 'body blow' to the He 219/Jumo 213E test programme. Fortunately for them, Oloff and Fischer made successful ejections and landed safely. This was Fischer's fourth parachute descent of the war, and as was becoming almost the norm, I./NJG 1 was unable to claim any victories in return.

The USAAF returned to Münster-Handorf on 21 March when 129 B-17s dropped more than 1000 bombs on the airfield and its environs. By the end of the raid, the airfield's runway had been cratered, its lighting system knocked out, five He 219s destroyed and a further seven damaged. The *Gruppe*'s war diary noted that 'flying was now out of the question'. Two days later, Münster-Handorf was again subjected to a prolonged bombing and strafing attack by USAAF P-47s. In the face of this, and when combined with the damage done on the 21st (the two attacks had destroyed a total of seven He 219s of the 20 that were hit), the decision was taken that I./NJG 1 should abandon the airfield and move to a safer haven further north.

On 29 March, I./NJG 1 left Münster-Handorf for the last time, with 30 of its remaining He 219s transferring to Bremen-Neulanderfeld. During this move (which was temporary), Feldwebel Günther Thurow and his bordfunker, Unteroffizier Neff, ground looped G9+WH at Neulanderfeld when their aircraft hit a bomb crater, while the He 219 being flown by 8./NJG 1's Unteroffizier Adam Holl and his bordfunker, Feldwebel Helmut Walter, was shot down by marauding USAAF fighters. By 31 March I./NJG 1 had moved (via Nordholz, on the north German coast) to the airfield of Westerland, on the island of Sylt. On 3 April, the surviving

CHAPTER FOUR **ENDGAME**

technical facilities and installations at Münster-Handorf were demolished and the base abandoned.

The end of March 1945 also saw the Luftwaffe's *Inspekteur der Nachtjagd* (Inspector of Nightfighters) Oberst Werner Streib institute a scheme whereby all the service's *Nachtjagdgeschwader* bar NJG 2 were to reduce each of their *Gruppen* to single *Staffel*-sized units, with each 'new' *Staffel* having a strength of 16 aircraft and 26 crews. At the same time, all aircrew who were not deemed to be *Spitzenbesatzungen* were to be either used to fly ground-support missions or be redirected as 'cannon fodder' elsewhere within the *Wehrmacht* (armed forces). As a result of this, I./NJG 1's first, second and third *Staffeln* were merged into a 'new' 1./NJG 1.

As April 1945 opened, *Luftflotte Reich* reported 1./NJG 1 having 12 He 219s, NJG 1's *Stabstaffel* having 27 assorted Bf 110s and He 219s and NJG 3 having 61 assorted Bf 110s, Ju 88s and He 219s. Of these, the Westerland-based 1./NJG 1 was reporting that its fuel situation was such as to preclude any current flight operations.

Further information is provided by the survey of Luftwaffe airfields undertaken by Spitfire PR XI photo-reconnaissance aircraft of the RAF's No 16 Sqn between 2 April and 4 May. The flights determined that between

He 219A-7 Wk-Nr 310106 is the only He 219 known to the author that was retrofitted with the FuG 218 *Neptun* AI radar in place of the FuG 220 set. This view clearly shows the smaller (when compared with that used with the SN 2 equipment) dipole array associated with *Neptun*, and it should be noted that this aircraft was also fitted with the FuG 350 *Naxos* centimetric radar homing device. At the end of the war in Europe, Wk-Nr 310106 was brought to Britain for evaluation, where it was given the Air Ministry number 44 (*EN Archive*)

four and ten He 219s were present at Bremen-Neulanderfeld airfield, one at Lübeck-Blankensee, six at Lüneberg, one at Parchim, one at Nordholz, between five and six at Schwerin, between two and five at Ludwigslust, between four and 11 at Westerland and single examples at Flensburg-Schäferhaus, Schleswig-Jagel, Husum and Copenhagen-Kastrup.

In mid-April, IX. *(J) Luftwaffenkommando West* reported 1./NJG 1 as having 22 He 219s (16 of which were serviceable) and the *Geschwader*'s *Stabstaffel* 28 (12 serviceable) Bf 110s and He 219s. Mention has also been made of 7./NJG 5 having 16 (12 serviceable) He 219s and Ju 88s at this time. Aside from such strength returns, the author has been unable to find any additional data on NJG 5's posited use of the He 219. This said, he believes that the unit probably did have examples of the aircraft on strength during 1945.

As if the foregoing reorganisation and fragmentation of the available He 219 inventory was not enough, further disruption was engendered by an April 1945 attempt to recapitalise the Luftwaffe's AI radar capability, with the FuG 218 *Neptun* equipment being designated to replace the now heavily compromised FuG 220. Following successful trials of the new equipment by NJG 4, this replacement process was at least begun, with NJG 1 being slated to receive approximately 35 such radars with which to retrofit its aircraft. At least one Heinkel nightfighter (He 219A-7 Wk-Nr 310106, which was at Westerland at war's end) is confirmed as having been so equipped.

Returning to specifically identified He 219 activity, Feldwebel Günther Thurow and his bordfunker, Unteroffizier Neff, are known to have made an 84-minute-long daylight flight from Bremen-Neulanderfeld in G9+CH in early April. 1./NJG 1 scrambled three of its aircraft at 2145 hrs on 8–9 April to oppose an RAF raid on Hamburg. Of these, the Modrow/Schneider crew were in G9+HH and Baake and his bordfunker in G9+AB. The third aircraft (flown by Major Alfred Hemm) experienced radio problems and returned to base 30 minutes after taking off. The *Staffel*'s war diary records that the raid was thought to have been against Lübeck, and that Modrow's SN 2 radar was 'completely jammed'.

As April 1945 progressed, 1./NJG 1's paper strength appeared to have stabilised at 22, with an additional aircraft (19 rather than 18) being serviceable on the 9th. Three days later, *Luftflotte Reich* was confirming 1./NJG 1 and NJG 1's *Stabstaffel* as having 22 He 219s and 28 Bf 110s/He 219s, respectively, and it was again noting 7./NJG 5 as having 16 Ju 88s and He 219s.

On 13 April, Wk-Nr 190226 (which had been shot up at Flensburg when it made an emergency landing there on the night of 5–6 April) was 80 per cent damaged at that base due to enemy action. That He 219s were still transferring to Westerland in dribs and drabs is illustrated by the fact that Feldwebel Thurow and his bordfunker made a transfer flight aboard G9+HL from Ludwigslust to Westerland between 2048–2229 hrs on 18 April.

For only the second time that month, the night of 19–20 April saw 1./NJG 1 back in combat when it scrambled seven He 219s from Westerland. Along with 34 other *Zahme Sau* aircraft from other *Nachtjagdgeschwader*, the *Staffel* opposed RAF Bomber Command's combined raids on Hamburg and Lützkendorf, a diversionary attack on Travemünde and three small Mosquito strikes on Berlin and Dessau.

At 2145 hrs, the 41 fighters were instructed to fly towards Hamburg, with 2150 hrs seeing some of then re-directed to the *Quelle* (water spring) beacon at Henmoor on Germany's north coast. The first vectors into the bomber 'stream' were given at around 2209 hrs, with the Travemünde diversion now being thought to be the main target. The first bombs dropped on Travemünde at 2220 hrs, and all available fighters were sent there between 2225–2230 hrs. The general confusion is reflected in 1./NJG 1's war diary that recorded the night's raid as being a '4-motor attack on Lübeck'. At 2230 hrs, Hamburg was finally recognised as a target, and ten minutes later, all available aircraft were ordered to fly to that city. The raid on Lützkendorf, in southeast Germany, was all but ignored until 2246 hrs, when the first fighters from NJG 5 were sent there – two minutes after the attack had opened.

Of the 1./NJG 1 contingent, Hauptmann Modrow was flying G9+EH, while the mission represented Unteroffizier Erich Schneider's 103rd and final operational sortie of the war. Modrow's bordfunker, Feldwebel Bettaque, noted it as his 118th operational sortie, and the flight had generated a brief visual contact, failure of his FuG 220 AI radar and a landing at Westerland through a 30 m cloud base. Less fortunate than both Schneider and Modrow, Hauptmann Graf Rosséguier de Miremont (in He 219A-2 Wk-Nr 420328 G9+OL) was shot up by a No 151 Sqn Mosquito NF XXX flown by Flt Lt W A Lindsay (pilot) and Flg Off P Signey (radar operator/navigator). Lindsay's combat report gives a vivid picture of the night's events;

'The aerodrome [Westerland] was lit up on arrival at 2245 hrs, so we patrolled in the neighbourhood. At 2310 hrs when at 1000 ft I had just turned away on a northeast course from the aerodrome when Flg Off Signey obtained a head-on contact, range four miles. I started a port orbit when the target flashed past at very close range, port to starboard. I turned behind him and Flg Off Signey regained contact at 1500 ft. Closed range on a gently weaving and climbing target and obtained a visual on the exhausts and then on the aircraft itself, which gave no "F" [an RAF infra-red identification device] response. Navigator then recognised target as He 219 through night glasses, and this I was able to confirm.

'In order to open fire, I weaved back to 300 ft and gave a short burst from dead astern. Strikes were seen on starboard wing root, followed by a vivid white flash. Immediately afterwards a shower of sparks came from the area of [the] explosion, obscuring my view of the target. I was now at about 3000 ft height and my navigator was able to follow [the] target, which was orbiting [to] starboard very tightly and losing height rapidly. I was only able to obtain fleeting visuals at this period. Contact was finally lost at 800 ft in ground returns, and despite [a] further search nothing more was seen.

'We then resumed patrol near the aerodrome, which had its lights doused and was firing intruder warnings [warning flares]. I claim an He 219 damaged.'

Rosséguier and his bordfunker, Feldwebel Bengel, were indeed lucky to survive this attack, which knocked out one of G9+OL's engines and damaged its wings and propellers. Rosséguier managed to make it back to Westerland, where he crash-landed on one engine. G9+OL suffered

He 219A-2 Wk-Nr 290126 was assigned Air Ministry number 20 and flown from Schleswig (where this photograph was taken) to RAE Farnborough on 3 August 1945. Eighteen days later it was transferred to the RAF's No 6 MU at Brize Norton. Subsequently, it was struck off charge during 1946 (*EN Archive*)

50–60 per cent damage in the incident. This dramatic combat was perhaps a fitting finale to the He 219's combat career, for this proved to be 1./NJG 1's last operational mission of World War 2.

As the situation around it deteriorated, 1./NJG 1 was ordered to disband on 30 April, with its personnel to now form part of the ground defence of Schleswig and Husum. Fortunately for those involved, they had not yet reached Husum when German forces in northwest Germany, the Netherlands and Denmark surrendered to the Allies on 5 May. Less fortunate was Westerland itself, which was subject to a 'Firebash' (napalm) attack by Mosquito fighter-bombers of the RAF's No 515 Sqn on the night of 2–3 May. Six days later, Germany capitulated, with all of its remaining military forces surrendering unconditionally. Although skirmishes continued over the next few days, World War 2 in Europe was finally over.

With such a concentration of He 219s in northwestern Germany, it is not surprising that a relatively large number of these aircraft fell into British hands, for this was the principal geographical area of British Army operations in Europe during the final months of the conflict.

At war's end, 45 He 219s (reportedly including Wk-Nrs 211120, 290117, 290123, 290196, 310106, 310112, 310182, 310188, 310204, 310208, 310215, 420328 and 420331) were captured at Westerland, with a further 25 (reportedly including Wk-Nrs 210903, 290202, 290126, 310109, 310189 and 310200, all of which were airworthy) being acquired at Grove. From these, five were taken to Britain (including, in known Wk-Nr order, 290126, 310106, 310109 and 310189), with three more (Wk-Nrs 290060, 290202 and 210903) being sent to the United States.

Looking at the British aircraft first, He 219A-2 Wk-Nr 290126 D5+BL was a 3./NJG 3 machine that was captured at Grove and given the Air Ministry (AM) number 20. Equipped with FuG 220 radar, D5+BL was transferred from Grove to Schleswig on 1 August 1945, before being flown to the Royal Aircraft Establishment (RAE) at Farnborough, in Hampshire, two days later. AM 20 is known to have been test flown on 7 August and ferried to No 6 Maintenance Unit (MU) at RAF Brize Norton, in Oxfordshire, two weeks later. It was struck off charge (SOC) during 1947.

For its part, He 219A-7 Wk-Nr 310106 (which was given the number AM 44) was the most interesting, for it was fitted with FuG 218 *Neptun* AI radar and a FuG 350 radar homer. AM 44 arrived at RAF Ford, in

West Sussex, on 24 June 1945 for assessment by the RAF's Night Fighter Development Wing. On 27 July it was transferred to RAF Tangmere, again, in West Sussex. It is reported to have had its radar evaluated (using RAF aircraft as targets) throughout the summer of 1945. AM 44 was transferred to Brize Norton on 19 October 1945 and was in store at No 6 MU until it was SOC on 14 August 1947.

Elsewhere, He 219A-7 Wk-Nr 310109 (which was allocated the number AM 21) was flown from Grove to Schleswig on 7 August 1945 and then on to RAE Farnborough five days later. Fitted with FuG 220 radar and (possibly) an example of the FuG 350 radar homer, it was declared surplus to requirements and transferred to No 51 MU for scrapping in January 1948. Originally, it had been intended to preserve this aircraft as a museum exhibit.

The RAF's last positively identified example (He 219A-2 Wk-Nr 310189 D5+CL) was another NJG 3 aircraft which was given the AM number 22. Equipped with FuG 220 AI radar, AM 22 was flown from Schleswig to RAE Farnborough on 27 August 1945 and displayed at the German Aircraft Exhibition that allowed the British public to see a selection of Luftwaffe aircraft at Farnborough between 29 October and 9 November 1945. Sadly, AM 22 ended up on Farnborough's scrap heap, where it was logged during December 1946.

The remaining He 219 brought to Britain is something of a 'mystery ship'. Variously identified as AM 43 and AM 45 (which was, in fact, a Ju 188), this aircraft was captured at Westerland and had at least one fin and rudder from He 219A-7 Wk-Nr 310114. Whatever this aircraft's model or its previous identity, the He 219 was present at RAF Ford circa August 1945. The confusion over its identity probably arises from the initial British instruction that all captured He 219s should have their propellers, fins and rudders removed to prevent unauthorised flights while on the Continent. When the decision to bring a particular airframe back to full serviceability was made, it did not necessarily receive its original components during the re-build.

Air Ministry number 22 (He 219A-2 Wk-Nr 310189) was brought to RAE Farnborough on 27 August 1945 and put on display as part of that establishment's exhibition of German aircraft staged between 29 October and 9 November 1945. Like all other He 219s flown to Britain, it was unceremoniously scrapped (and logged as such at Farnborough) during December 1946 (*EN Archive*)

For their part, the trio of He 219s that went to the United States were all originally captured by the British at Grove. He 219A-0 Wk-Nr 210903 (which was given the USAAF serial FE-612, which was later amended to T2-612) had been delivered to II./NJG 1 in May 1944 and given the *Verbandekenzeichen* G9+LP. Transferred from Deelen to Venlo, G9+LP went on to serve with I./NJG 1 (from 11 July 1944) prior to being captured and sent to the United States aboard the British aircraft carrier HMS *Reaper* in July 1945. As T2-612, and equipped with FuG 220 AI radar, the aircraft was placed in storage at Freeman Field, Indiana, on 17 May 1946 and eventually scrapped during 1950.

Wk-Nr 290060 was an He 219A-2 that was given the USAAF serial FE-613/T2-613 – it had originally been marked up by its British captors as 'USA 9'. This aircraft was handed over to the USAAF on 26 June 1945 and flown to Cherbourg by Capt Fred McIntosh for onward shipment to the United States. FE-613/T2-613 was another FuG 220-equipped aircraft, and it appears to have been used as a source of spares for FE-614/T2-614. The nightfighter was placed in storage at Freeman Field during August 1946 and eventually scrapped.

The remaining American example (He 219A-2 Wk-Nr 290202, USAAF serial FE-614/T2-614) is perhaps the most interesting in that it survived into the 21st century, has been fully restored and as of 2026 formed part of the National Air and Space Museum's (NASM) Udvar-Hazy collection. Wk-Nr 290202 was flown to Cherbourg by German pilot Heinz Braun (under American tutelage) on 27 June 1945, where it joined the others of its kind aboard HMS *Reaper* for the trip across the Atlantic.

Once in the United States, the nightfighter was ferried from Newark, New Jersey, to Freeman Field. During the summer of 1946, it underwent work to make it airworthy. This was 90 per cent completed by 1 August, when it was decided that it should become a museum exhibit. On 17 September, the He 219 was shipped to Park Ridge, Illinois, for museum preservation, being handed over to the NASM in Washington, DC, during 1951. FE-614/T2-614 was dismantled in 1960 and placed in

The He 219A-0, A-2, A-7 and D-1 all utilised a common airframe, as exemplified by this side view of He 219A-0 Wk-Nr 210903 when it was one of three examples of the Heinkel nightfighter under evaluation in the US post-May 1945. Given the USAAF serial FE-612, which was later amended to T2-612, this aircraft had been delivered new to II./NJG 1 in May 1944 and given the G9+LP. It finished the war assigned to I./NJG 1 and was eventually scrapped during 1950 (*EN Archive*)

This view of the interior of the rear fuselage of He 219A-2 Wk-Nr 290202 clearly illustrates that it offered more than enough room to accommodate an observer/gunner as a third crewman. The aircraft, which is part of the NASM collection, was in fact field-modified with a rear-looking viewing point for a third crewmen in the rear fuselage (*EN Archive*)

long-term storage prior to the decision being made to give it a complete restoration in preparation for the aircraft's public display as part of the NASM collection.

Wk-Nr 290202 is something of a composite, for it is fitted with the fins and rudders from Wk-Nr 290060. During restoration, the aircraft was discovered to be one of the He 219s that were field-modified with a rear-looking viewing point for a third crewman in the rear fuselage.

Alongside the described British and American evaluations, the Soviet Red Army captured anywhere between one and three He 219s as it swept westward in the final stages of the war in the east. Russian sources identify one captured He 219 as having been the subject of a summer 1945 letter from the then People's Commissar of the Aircraft Industry, Aleksey I Shakhoorin, to the Communist Party's Central Committee, and it is presumed that the Heinkel was of interest due to its radar and crew ejection system. It is also suggested

In this view of the bordfunker's equipment rack in the rear of the He 219's cockpit, it is obvious that the currently preserved He 219A-2 Wk-Nr 290202 was at some point fitted with American electronics to facilitate 'safety of flight' in the US during its post-war evaluation. The photograph depicts the aircraft when it was in long-term storage prior to its restoration to museum exhibit standard (*EN Archive*)

Despite its indifferent quality, this historically interesting photograph shows one of the two He 219s that were supplied to the then Czechoslovakia by the then Soviet Union during 1946. Both aircraft are understood to have been scrapped in late 1952 (*EN Archive*)

that captured documentation threw further light on the He 219, the earlier and ultra-streamlined He 119 and the proposed He 419 development of the basic He 219 design.

The Russians are also credited as having passed two He 219s (one of which, coded white 34, is confirmed photographically) to then Czechoslovakia during 1946. One of these is reported to have been overhauled by the Czech aviation company Letov during 1950, and once airworthy, to have been briefly used by the Czech *Výkunný technický letecký ústav* (Military Technical Air Institute) for ejector seat trials. Subsequently, it (together with a second He 219) was turned over to the Czech Air Force, where it was designated as a *Lenka Bombardovaci 79* (light bomber 79). Both aircraft are understood to have been scrapped in late 1952.

At this point, it seems sensible to try and pass judgement on the success or failure of the He 219 as a nightfighter. In the 80 years since the end of World War 2, few of the Luftwaffe's wartime aircraft have been mythologised to the extent that the He 219 has, with some describing it as that service's most potent night interceptor, while others (accepting that it was 'excellent in concept') brand it as having been underpowered and difficult to handle in certain flight regimes. In this regard, there were significant wartime protagonists both for and against the aircraft, with the Luftwaffe's Generalmajor Dietrich Peltz being a good representative of the 'pro' camp, while the RAE's Capt Eric 'Winkle' Brown stands out for the 'against' lobby.

For his part, Peltz flew a new Schwechat-produced He 219 during May 1944, reporting that it had made a 'great impression' on him, and that he had not realised how 'good' the type was, particularly when compared with Messerschmitt's Me 410. Again, he judged it to be easy to fly, that it flew 'as well on one engine as most types [did] on two', that its stall warning attributes were 'adequate', that it had the 'smoothness' of the Ju 188 and that it was easier to land than the Me 410. Peltz ended his review with the observation that with the declining quality of pilots then coming through the Luftwaffe's training system, good flying, take-off and landing characteristics of the type shown by the He 219 should be 'decisive factors' in the Luftwaffe's choice of aircraft.

It is not clear whether Peltz flew a fully equipped He 219 or a 'green' airframe without such things as radar antennas and exhaust flame dampers installed.

For his part, the Royal Navy test pilot 'Winkle' Brown flew several of the He 219s that were brought to Britain post-May 1945. In his published account of flying the type, he prefaces his thoughts with the observation that the British did not carry out any specific performance or handling tests with the He 219, being only interested in 'certain items of equipment' (thought to centre on the FuG 218 radar and its ejector seat system) fitted aboard the aircraft. He then goes on to rate the He 219 as a 'six' on his scale of 'one' to 'ten' (with 'one' being the worst and 'ten' the best), and to describe it as being 'underpowered' and exhibiting poor longitudinal control at low speeds, where there was 'constant danger of stalling'.

In more detail, Brown states his belief that an engine failure during a night take-off in an He 219A-2 would have been a 'very nasty emergency', for below an airspeed of 220 km/h, the aircraft would have been very hard to keep straight and level. Furthermore, the 'sink' engendered when the aircraft's undercarriage was retracted would have put it in a 'coffin corner' at altitudes of between 15 m and 91 m. When landing, Brown noted that the aircraft's ailerons were 'sluggish', which suggested that turns with its flaps lowered were 'not to be recommended'. Again, he recorded that in gusty conditions the He 219 was 'unpleasant' to control laterally during final approach.

Brown summed up his report with the observation that the He 219's reputation was 'somewhat overrated', and that while being 'basically a good nightfighter in concept', the aircraft was underpowered, making certain flight attitudes difficult to handle. It should also be noted that the He 219s Brown flew were mostly equipped with radar antennas (or, at the very least, their support arms) and exhaust flame dampers.

At this remove, it is hard to say which of these viewpoints carries the most weight. Accordingly, is it possible to make any definitive judgements on the type's effectiveness or otherwise? From the author's research, it seems clear that the He 219 was not capable of intercepting RAF Mosquitos fitted with two-stage Merlin engines on a regular basis. Furthermore, there were

Generalmajor Dietrich Peltz, seen here as an Oberst, was a very experienced bomber pilot and highly decorated officer who flew a brand new He 219 on an evaluation flight in May 1944. Although it appears that his flying time in the aircraft was limited to this one sortie, it was enough to make him a firm supporter of the Heinkel nightfighter – Peltz was particularly impressed with the He 219's handling qualities and landing characteristics, both of which he judged to be superior to those of the Me 410 (*Robert Forsyth Collection*)

too few aircraft available to make a real impact, and that in all probability the He 219 was not fully developed until near the end of its service in May 1945.

On the plus side, its forward-firing armament of six 20/30 mm cannon (frequently augmented by a pair of 30 mm MK 108 *Schräge Musik* oblique-firing weapons) was devastatingly effective; the He 219 was the Luftwaffe's fastest piston-engined nightfighter of the European war; and its ejector seat system was both effective and a life saver in circumstances where there was a very good chance of the crew being killed.

Looking at the 'cons' first, the He 219A-0 (the most widely used variant) was just fast enough to catch a Mosquito B IV flying at a maximum speed of 612 km/h at 6096 m but it was not fast enough to get into a stern chase firing position against a two-stage Merlin-powered Mosquito B XVI flying at its maximum speed of 643 km/h at 7620 m. In fact, speed was probably not the major problem here but rather altitude. The He 219A-0's best performance was in the range 619 km/h at 6401 m to 585 km/h at 7,500 m, meaning that it was capable of catching a Mosquito B IV but not a late model of the de Havilland

Whilst serving as the commanding officer of 'Operation Enemy Flight', Lt Cdr Eric 'Winkle' Brown (then the chief naval test pilot at RAE Farnborough and a fluent German speaker) flew a number of captured Luftwaffe types such as the Arado Ar 234 jet bomber, seen here, and the He 219. Indeed, he completed flights in several of the Heinkel nightfighters brought to England, after which he stated the aircraft were underpowered. In Brown's view, he thought that although the He 219 was 'basically a good nightfighter', its reputation was 'somewhat overrated' (*Public Domain*)

bomber that was able to fly as much as 394 m higher and 58 km/h faster than an A-0, whose optimum speed performance was (according to its handbook) achievable at 6401 m.

The need for more powerful engines for the He 219 was not lost on the Germans, with the country's aviation industry proving incapable of series production of a reliable motor that was more powerful at higher altitudes than the DB 603A, DB 603AA and Jumo 213E (believed to have been fitted to one prototype and five 'production' examples) of operational He 219s. With regards to numbers (and during the aircraft's 24 months of service), I./NJG 1 seems never to have been able to put up more than 20 He 219s for any given operation, with the number available during the type's first seven months in combat being nearer one or two! With such numbers, it is not surprising that the *Gruppe* was not particularly successful against relatively small raids by fast-flying Mosquitos that could easily be lost in the vastness of the skies over Germany and occupied Europe.

In terms of development, the same basic airframe was used in all the operational He 219 models. In service, the type was the subject of a litany of complaints that included unintentional undercarriage retractions; flap operation problems; leaking fuel tanks; inadequate cockpit heating; radiator and oil cooler failures; hydraulic line chaffing; the need to strengthen the aircraft's fuselage; poor flame damper installations; and unreliable AI radar. Of course, all new types have 'bugs' that need to be worked out, but in the case of the He 219, there is a sense that the design was not completely 'frozen' at the time of its service entry. Furthermore, the type appears to have suffered reduced component reliability and availability as Germany's military and industrial situation deteriorated during 1944–45.

With regard to its all-important AI radar, the He 219 entered service fitted with the FuG 202/212, which was effectively jammed by the RAF's *Window* resonating countermeasure from July 1943. Despite this, a FuG 212 variant had to be retained to augment the new FuG 220 SN 2 set which, although initially unjammed by *Window*, had inadequate close-range resolution for successful night interception when first used by I./NJG 1. While this problem was overcome, FuG 220 SN 2 was in turn jammed using so-called 'long' *Window*. This issue was only eradicated on a very limited scale by the introduction of the FuG 218 *Neptun* AI radar (which worked on a different frequency to FuG 220) at the end of the war.

It is also worth noting that while a tail-warning capability was developed for SN 2, it seems not to have been particularly widely applied to the He 219, resulting in the nightfighter being more vulnerable to attacks by Mosquito intruders than it should have been. Equally sparse was the installation of the FuG 350 *Naxos* radar homer (only three He 219 fits being known) which proved so successful in tracking British bomber 'streams' aboard aircraft such as the Ju 88G-6.

As set out in Chapter One, the He 219 was the subject of repeated attempts to halt its production. The cause of the animus towards the He 219 in certain quarters of the RLM remains unclear, but it may well have been partly due to Heinkel's fall from grace over the problems encountered with the disastrous He 177 heavy bomber programme. A similar lack of trust was encountered by Messerschmitt after the failure of its Me 210 *Zerstörer* (heavy fighter).

It is also clear that the He 219 was not liked by a number of *Nachtjagd* crews, who baulked at a two-man crew and the position of the aircraft's cockpit relative to its engines in case of the need to bail out. Indeed, a number of operational He 219s were jury-rigged with a position for an observer/gunner in their rear fuselages. Again, Heinkel was aware of this, and designed the He 219A-5 model which featured a three-man cockpit with provision for a rear gunner.

For the statistically minded, modern research posits that between June 1943 and May 1945, He 219 crews claimed the destruction of at least 150 enemy aircraft – a figure that includes ten Mosquitos and at least 100 four-engined bombers. During the course of its two years of service, approximately 100 He 219s were lost to enemy action, 'friendly fire' and accidents, with others being blown up on the ground by retreating German forces during the last days of the war in Europe.

At least 25 crewmen made successful ejections from stricken He 219s, with several doing so on multiple occasions. There is little doubt that the He 219's ejection system was one of its most successful features, and the Luftwaffe attempted to keep it secret for as long as possible. Indeed, it is probable that this ejection system was the reason for much of the post-war evaluation of the type, with its other equipment (and indeed its airframe) being somewhat *passé* at a time when AI radar was dominated by centimetric technology and the turbojet represented the future of aero engine development. Nonetheless, the He 219 was an imposing and striking looking warplane, and one which occupies a particular niche in the history of World War 2.

As a final point, it is worth noting that the frequently voiced assertion that the He 219 was one of the very few World War 2 aircraft specifically designed for the nightfighter role is incorrect, as is the He 219 having been given the name *Uhu*. The He 219 was conceived as a multi-role aircraft which was finally *adapted* for night interception. It was, indeed, the Luftwaffe's only nightfighter to be *produced* solely for the role, but it was not originally designed for it, with that accolade going to the American Northrop P-61 Black Widow and the Japanese Aichi S1A *Denko* (Lightning). The P-61 saw operational service in Europe, the Mediterranean and the Pacific, while the two prototype *Denko* fighters that were built were destroyed in USAAF B-29 raids on the Japanese home islands during 1945. Neither example was ever flown.

As to the *Uhu* name, the only *official* use of such a designation referred to either the Focke-Wulf Fw 189 short-range reconnaissance aircraft or the FuG 135 data transmission system.

CHAPTER FIVE

ANATOMY

During its 24 months of frontline service with the Luftwaffe, the He 219 was fielded in three operational (He 219A-0, A-2 and A-7) and one developmental (He 219 V41/He 219D-1) variants. All four shared a common airframe derived from that used in the He 219 V7 through V12 inclusive, and which differed from the type's first prototype by virtue of the introduction of a 940 mm longer, more streamlined fuselage, larger fins and rudders, extended engine nacelles and a revised cockpit canopy profile.

The fuselage of the He 219 V1 incorporated dorsal and ventral 'steps' (a hangover from the time when the type was intended to have remotely controlled gun barbettes for defence) and a cockpit canopy that was shaped to accommodate a rearward-firing weapon. The use of this 'standard' airframe facilitated main component interchange between the three primary operational variants, as was evidenced when the RAF 'mixed and matched' fins and rudders to make aircraft airworthy for the trip to England post-May 1945.

This 'standard' airframe took the form of a high-wing monoplane with underslung engine nacelles and twin fins and rudders mounted on horizontal tail surfaces that featured upward dihedral. Excluding any installed nose or tail antennas, the He 219 had an overall length of 15.54 m and was approximately 4.40 m off the ground at its highest point. The aircraft had a wingspan of 18.50 m and a total wing area of 44.50 m². It was equipped with a tricycle undercarriage that had a main wheel track of 5.00 m. In its

Prior to He 219A-019, all examples of the Heinkel nightfighter were fitted with the bulged cockpit canopy shown in this illustration taken from the He 219A-0's technical manual. This shape was intended to provide accommodation for a rear-firing weapon which, in the event, was never fitted (*EN Archive*)

From aircraft He 219A-019 onward, all Heinkel nightfighters were fitted with a canopy shaped as shown in this photograph of He 219A-2 Wk-Nr 290202, which, as of 2025, had been restored to museum standard for display in the NASM's Steven F. Udvar-Hazy Center. The view also illustrates the head rests for the type's ejector seats, together with the twin display screens for the FuG 220 SN 2 AI radar (*EN Archive*)

A-0 form, the He 219 had an empty weight of 8490 kg (± 1.5 per cent). For the same variant, the type's equipment weight (including communications equipment, flares, crew and fuel) was 9570 kg, giving a loaded weight of 12,260 kg.

The aircraft's pilot and bordfunker were seated back-to-back beneath a clear view canopy, with the cockpit being in the aircraft's nose. The crew were protected by both nose armour and an internal, 64 mm thick, bullet-proof windscreen ahead of the pilot. In more detail, this armoured windscreen has been described as having incorporated fine heating wires, and when looking forward, ended 101 mm away from the starboard side of the aircraft's curved outer windscreen.

A general view of the pilot's cockpit in an He 219A-0. The general arrangement of the instrumentation in the aircraft was deemed to be good, as was the pilot's view from the cockpit (*EN Archive*)

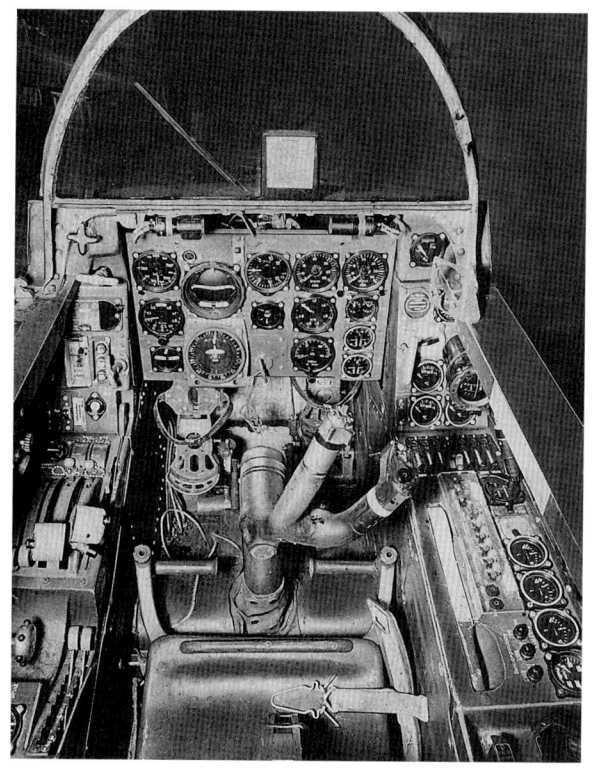

Both crewmen were seated on compressed air-driven ejector seats. The necessary pressurised gas and pistons were contained in a pair of cylinders that were positioned between the crew seats, with the starboard one serving the pilot and the port one the bordfunker. The pilot's cylinder was pressurised to 90 atmospheres, while that for the bordfunker's registered between 70 and 72 atmospheres. Both crew could jettison the canopy for egress, and the seats were equipped with footrests that ensured the crewmen's legs were tucked in in such a way as to clear their respective instrument and equipment panels when ejecting. Again, both the pilot's and the bordfunker's seats had headrests, with the pilot's example having to be in the upright position to avoid injuring the bordfunker in the event of ejection. When ejecting, the bordfunker is believed to have exited first.

As already noted, the Germans surrounded the He 219's ejection system with considerable secrecy throughout the type's operational life, and it was perhaps the most interesting aspect of the aircraft for the Allies. System design began in 1941, with trials involving graduated ground and air tests which culminated in the first human ejection that was made

The He 219 was among the first combat aircraft to be fitted with ejector seats. Operated by compressed air, the pilot's and radar/radio operator's seats are shown here undergoing, it is thought, examination at RAE Farnborough during the summer of 1945 (*EN Archive*)

by Rechlin test parachutist Wilhelm Buss. During its development process, problems were encountered with seat trajectories outside the aircraft – a shortcoming that was resolved by installing slightly curved driving pistons.

Between October 1943 and June 1944 (when the system was deemed to have passed its official test programme), 55 ejections were carried out from two He 219 testbeds (He 219 V6 Wk-Nr 190006 and He 219A-042 Wk-Nr 190113), and the system was first used operationally on 11–12 April 1944 by 2./NJG 1's Unteroffizier Herter and his bordfunker, Gefreiter Perbix, two months before it was officially cleared for service. Modern research suggests that at least 25 He 219 crewmen made successful ejections using this system, with the figure being possibly as high as 33.

He 219A-042 Wk-Nr 190113 DV+DI was one of two He 219s that were used to test the type's ejector seat system. This still from a chase aeroplane film shows what is believed to be a dummy being ejected (*EN Archive*)

The second aircraft to be used in the ejector seat development programme was the He 219 V6 Wk-Nr 190006. The last example of the type to be built with a 'short' fuselage, the aircraft was used for both ejector seat and radio equipment testing during August–September 1944. Note its modified canopy, which left the rear ejector seat location open to the elements (*EN Archive*)

The efficacy of the system is well illustrated by a number of crewmen making multiple successful ejections, with the record being held by Feldwebel Staffa, who exited doomed He 219s by ejector seat on no fewer than three occasions!

The He 219 made use of B4 (87 octane) fuel, with the A-0 carrying 2590 litres in forward, middle and rear tanks in its centre fuselage.

In terms of avionics, the three operational He 219 variants were equipped with a uniform fit that comprised the FuG 202/212 *Lichtenstein* BC/C-1, FuG 218 *Neptun* and FuG 220 *Lichtenstein* SN 2 AI radars; the 300 to 600 kHz band FuG 10 P communications and navigation radio; the 38.4 to 42.4 MHz band FuG 16 ZE or ZY very high frequency communications and control transceiver; the 117 to 133 MHz (123 to 128 MHz according to one source) band FuG 25 A identification friend-or-foe transponder; the 30 to 33.33 MHz band and 38 MHz spot frequency FuBl 2 blind-landing system; the 337 to 400 MHz band FuG 101 radio altimeter and the FuG 350 Z *Naxos* centimetric radar homing device that operated against 2.5 to 3.8 GHz emitters such as the RAF's *H2S* blind bombing and navigation radar.

According to the He 219A-0's handbook (and when fitted with FuG 220 radar), these core elements were augmented by an ADb 11/16 ZE junction box, an AFN 2 homing indicator, an EZ 6 homing receiver (part of the FuG 10 P fit), FBG 2, 3 and 213 remote control units (for the FuBl 2's EBl 3 F receiver, the FuG 10 P radio and the SN 2 AI radar, respectively), an HU 220 hand controller (for the FuG 220 radar), a PTK/p-2 radio compass and the SChK 17 and 213 switch boxes (with the latter forming part of the FuG 220 system). All these, plus the SG 212 (FuG 212) and SG 213 (FuG 220) radar displays, the FuG 10 P's E 10 aK receiver, the FuG 16 radio and the FuG 10 P's S 10 K and L transmitters were, for the most part, mounted in a 'block' that was attached to the rear bulkhead of the aircraft's cockpit.

Taken from the He 219A-0's technical manual, this image shows the layout of the bordfunker's equipment attached in a 'block' to the rear wall of the aircraft's cockpit. The left-hand display at the top of the 'block' is for the FuG 212 AI radar, while that to the right is for the FuG 220 set (*Author's Collection*)

It should also be noted that FuG 101, FuG 218 and FuG 350 installations aboard He 219s were rare, with only three or four being known to have been fitted with FuG 350 and only one with the FuG 218 AI radar (see following).

Looking at the various AI radars in more detail, the first He 219s were fitted with the FuG 202 equipment, which was superseded by the refined *Lichtenstein* C-1 produced between June and November 1943. A wide-angle FuG 212 variant was retained when the baseline 91 MHz *Lichtenstein* SN 2 set was introduced due to the latter's poor close-up target resolution. Once this was resolved (post April–May 1944), FuG 220 became the He 219's primary radar sensor, and it was equipped for tail-warning at a later stage in its life. SN 2 with tail-warning seems to have been mainly the prerogative of the He 219A-7.

At the very end of the war, it was the Luftwaffe's intention to replace FuG 220 with the 158 to 187 MHz band FuG 218 *Neptun* radar which, to date (2026), appears to have only been fitted to one aircraft. FuG 202/212 operated on a frequency of 490 MHz and had a maximum detection range of 2800 m. Alongside the baseline 91 MHz spot frequency FuG 220

A close-up of the nose of an He 219 equipped with a FuG 220 AI radar that operated on a frequency and wavelength of 73 MHz and 4.1 m respectively, and which was identified by the *VI* code on the aircraft's nose. While it has been suggested that the 45-degree arrangement of the set's antenna dipoles was designed to overcome Allied jamming, the author believes that it is more likely to have been a measure to ensure that the size of the dipoles needed to operate on the given frequency/wavelength was such as to make oblique installation necessary to afford adequate ground clearance (*EN Archive*)

(identified by the code *IV* normally applied to the He 219's nose), later sets of the type operated on a frequency of 73 MHz and were identified by the code *VI*. Generic FuG 220 had a maximum range of 8000 m against a four-engined bomber, with FuG 218 offering 7000 m against a similar target.

Throughout its life, the He 219 had provision for a forward-firing armament of up to six cannon, with the weapons mounted in its wings (two 20 mm Mauser MG 151/20s) and a ventral fairing that could accommodate up to four MG 151/20s, four 30 mm Rheinmetall-Borsig MK 103 or four 30 mm Rheinmetall-Borsig MK 108 cannon. Use of the MK 103 (which had a rate-of-fire and muzzle velocity of 450 rounds per minute and 860 m per second, respectively) seems to have been rare. The MK 108 *Presslufthammer* (Jackhammer) had a muzzle velocity and rate-of-fire of 525 m per second and 600 rounds per minute respectively.

Using *Minen Geschoß* (literally 'mine bullet') high-powered ammunition, the MK 108 required just four rounds to mortally damage or destroy a four-engined bomber. In addition to forward-firing MK 108s, many He 219s were fitted with an additional pair of such weapons installed so as to fire obliquely upwards from the aircraft's fuselage (the *Schräge Musik* fit).

Turning to the differences between the four variants that were used operationally, 121 He 219A-0s were produced at Schwechat and Rostock-Marienehe between July 1943 and June 1944. Essentially a

When first introduced on the He 219, the SN 2 AI radar had very poor close-in resolution, which meant it had to be augmented by a wide-angle application of the FuG 212 set that resulted in the complex antenna array shown here. This aircraft has frequently been identified as having belonged to NJGr 10, although that has never been confirmed. The muzzle for the MG 151/20 20 mm cannon mounted in the port wing root is clearly visible (*EN Archive*)

preproduction run, these A-0s were identified by sequential numbers, with the first example being designated as the A-01 and so on. Again, the He 219A-0 was powered by a pair of Daimler-Benz DB 603A liquid-cooled, inline engines (driving three-bladed propellers) which offered climb/combat ratings of 1558 hp at sea level, 1647 hp at 2100 m and 1489 hp at 5700 m.

During the 12 months the A-0 was in production, a series of modifications were introduced, with the He 219A-019 being the first to be fitted with a redesigned cockpit canopy (in place of the original 'bulged' unit); the He 219A-061 being the first to feature revised wing leading edge air intakes; the He 219A-074 being the first to be fitted with FuG 16 ZY radio in place of the FuG 16 ZE equipment; and the He 219A-094 being the first to be fitted with single core electrical wiring. Elsewhere, some of these aircraft may also have been fitted with two 30 mm MK 108 cannon in a *Schräge Musik* installation and formed part of the effort to provide a rear fuselage viewing panel for an observer to give warning of attacks from astern.

The next major service variant was the He 219A-2, which made use of the A-0 airframe and the refined canopy that was fitted to aircraft from the He 219A-019 onward. Other introductions included oblique *Schräge Musik* weapons, single core electrical cabling and the DB 603AA engine (again, driving three-bladed propellers). The DB 603AA differed from the DB 603A in being fitted with a *großer Lader* (literally, 'large loader', with a better contextual translation being 'large charger') single-stage supercharger which offered a maximum boost altitude of 7300 m. DB 603AA climb/combat ratings are given as having been 1489 hp at sea level, 1548 hp at 1800 m and 1351 hp at 7200 m.

The He 219 was equipped with a tricycle undercarriage that comprised the nosewheel and twin wheel main undercarriage units that are shown here on an He 219A-0 captured intact at Bindbach, near Bayreuth, when the airfield was taken by 11th Armored Division of the US 3rd Army. Other points of interest are the four gun ports for the underfuselage MG 151/20 20 mm cannon and the considerable height of the He 219's cockpit when it was sitting on the ground (*Public Domain*)

Unconfirmed (but believed to be reasonably accurate) specification/performance data for the He 219A-2 includes empty and loaded weights of 8120 kg and 12,500 kg, respectively, a range of 1900 km at cruising power, a maximum speed of 585 km/h at 7500 m and a service ceiling of 8900 m.

A total of 100 He 219A-2s are understood to have been built at Schwechat (15 examples) and Rostock-Marienehe between July–December 1944. Like the He 219A-0, the A-2 was the subject of modification during its production life, with an example being the installation on some late production aircraft of the 390-litre engine nacelle fuel tanks that were a standard feature of the He 219A-7.

Aside from these extra tanks, the A-7 (which made use of the A-2's airframe) was fitted with DB 603E engines. Entering production in late July 1944, the DB 603E differed from the DB 603AA by virtue of its redesigned (and larger) gearbox and the introduction of an *ölschleuder* (oil slinger) that improved engine lubrication. The DB 603E's climb/combat ratings are given as 1558 hp at sea level, 1627 hp at 1800 m and 1420 hp at 7100 m. In all, Rostock-Marienehe are believed to have produced some 100 He 219A-7s between December 1944 and March 1945.

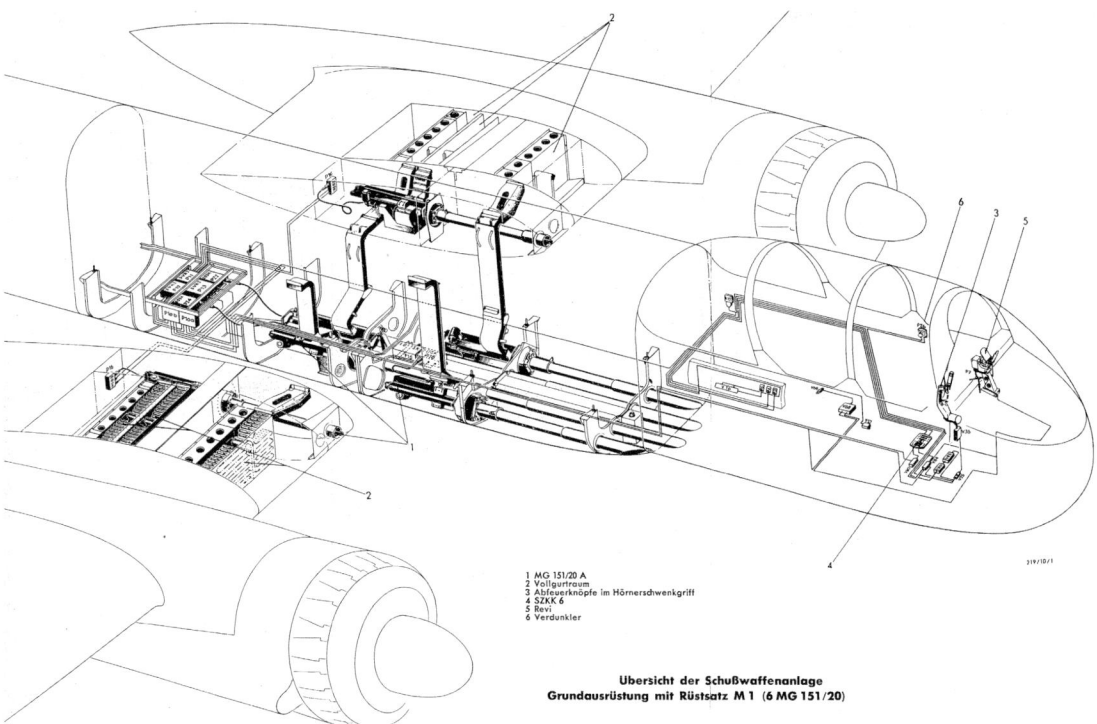

1 MG 151/20 A
2 Vollgurtraum
3 Abfeuerknöpfe im Hörnerschwenkgriff
4 SZKK 6
5 Revi
6 Verdunkler

**Übersicht der Schußwaffenanlage
Grundausrüstung mit Rüstsatz M 1 (6 MG 151/20)**

A diagram from the He 219A-0's technical manual that shows the layout of the aircraft's forward-firing armament. Note the location of the necessary ammunition magazines within the wings of the nightfighter (*EN Archive*)

The final He 219 model to appear (with only one prototype and five production aircraft being built) was the He 219D-1, which lacked a *Schräge Musik* installation and was powered by Jumo 213E/F engines. The E and F Jumo 213s differed from one another by virtue of the F's ability to be augmented by the MW 50 methanol and water injection system that was designed to increase engine output over short periods.

For its part, the Jumo 213E offered a climb/combat rating of 1558 hp at sea level and an emergency rating of 1302 hp at 9600 m. Based on the He 219A-2 airframe, the first Jumo 213 installation was aboard the He 219 V41 Wk-Nr 420325, with the five production D-1s being produced at Schwechat between January–March 1945. As far as is known, only the He 219 V41 was used operationally prior to its loss on 21–22 February 1945.

The out-of-sequence designations used for the four described models is accounted for by Heinkel's enthusiastic design of 'better' He 219s that were, at best, prototyped or at worst, never left the drawing board. The first of these paper designs was the He 219A-1 which seems to have been a proposed designation for aircraft fitted with the streamlined canopy shape introduced on the He 219A-019. Next in line was the He 219A-3, which was to have been powered by the DB 603E and to have featured 'miniaturised standard equipment' and (possibly) provision for a 900-litre drop tank.

The He 219A-4 was to have been a *Moskitojäger* (Mosquito hunter) that was a development of the A-2, had no provision for *Schräge Musik* weapons and was to be fitted with the GM-1 nitrous oxide power boosting system. GM-1 is known to have been tested on the He 219 V15 Wk-Nr 190064 and V32 Wk-Nr 190121. Of these, the V15 was also used as a testbed for

A typical He 219 *Schräge Musik* installation of two 30 mm MK 108 cannon as seen in the aircraft's rear fuselage, looking forward. He 219s appear to have been both built with and retrofitted with *Schräge Musik* weapons throughout 1944–45 (*Author's Collection*)

the FuG 16 ZY radio and the FuG 135 *Uhu* data transmission system, while the V32 underwent service trials.

The He 219A-5 is something of a 'mystery ship', as several sources suggest that it was put into production and delivered to the Luftwaffe. Other sources (which the author is inclined to believe) record it as being another 'paper' aeroplane that was based on the He 219A-3. What is on much firmer ground is the A-5 being a three-seat aircraft, with provision for a rear gunner in a raised and (almost) separate cockpit to those of his crew mates. The proposal's fuel capacity is given as having been 2590 litres housed in fuselage tanks and auxiliary tanks in the rear of each engine nacelle, and the aircraft was to be equipped with *Schräge Musik* weapons. The He 219 V34 Wk-Nr 190112 is reported to have been retained by Heinkel for conversion to a three-seat configuration.

The He 219A-6 was another *Moskitojäger* proposal that was to have been based on the A-2 airframe, with reduced armament and armour and powered by DB 603AAs. Again, the A-6 was not planned to incorporate a *Schräge Musik* installation.

CHAPTER FIVE **ANATOMY**

As applied to the He 219, the DB 603AA engine featured a novel radiator that saw its elements arranged around the powerplant's front section. In the He 219 fit, cooling air was drawn in from the front of the aircraft's engine nacelles (*EN Archive*)

In May 1944 Heinkel issued a flurry of works drawings that depicted an He 219 'second generation' which comprised the He 219B-1/B-2, C-1 and C-2. In order, the He 219B-1 was a three-seater that had a wingspan of 21.6 m, an enlarged undercarriage, two Jumo 222A/B engines (driving four-bladed propellers), an armament of two MG 151/20s in its wing roots, two MK 108s in a ventral tray and two more MK 108s in a *Schräge Musik* installation and a 3790-litre fuel load.

For its part, the Jumo 222 was a very compact, 24 cylinder, supercharged, liquid-cooled inline engine that offered 2465 hp for take-off and 1875 hp for cruise. This engine, together with the 21.6 m wing, were tested on the He 219 V16 (He 219A-079 Wk-Nr 190193), which made its maiden flight on 23 July 1944. The V16 had completed 12 test flights when, in November 1944, problems with one of the Jumo 222s grounded it. The V16's test programme was shut down on 2 January 1945, and the British are known to have captured a B-1 type 'long' wing when they occupied Schwechat in the summer of 1945. This unit featured a 4.9 m long aileron.

Elsewhere, the He 219 V27 has also been identified as being a B-1 prototype with a 'flattened canopy'. As of this writing, there is considerable doubt as to whether or not this aircraft was actually built, or, if it was, whether it was completed before May 1945.

The He 219B-2 *Höhenjäger* (high-altitude fighter) reverted to a two-man crew and was to be powered by DB 603s fitted with TK 13 exhaust-driven superchargers and driving three-bladed propellers. Again, the B-2 was to make use of a 22.6 m span 'long' wing, a beefed-up undercarriage, the B-1's fuel capacity and an armament that was to be made up of two MG 151/20s in its wing roots and a fuselage *Schräge Musik* installation.

Intended to power the He 219B-1 and C1 'paper' aeroplanes, the Jumo 222 was an extremely compact, high-powered, liquid-cooled engine that never achieved its initial promise and never entered serial production. Shown here is the Jumo 22E/F variant (*EN Archive*)

The He 219C-1 was another Jumo 222-powered project that made use of the B-1's fuselage (extended by 300 mm); a three-man, pressurised cockpit with staggered seating; a manned HL 131 V tail turret (fitted with four 13 mm MG 131 machine guns), two MG 151s in its wing roots, two MK 108s in a ventral tray and a *Schräge Musik* installation; a 3850-litre fuel capacity; an enlarged undercarriage; and four-bladed propellers. The He 219C-2 was a fighter-bomber version of the C-1 that dispensed with the latter's radar and *Schräge Musik* installation, featured a forward-firing armament of two MK 103 cannon and was to be capable of carrying three 500 kg SC 500 bombs beneath its fuselage.

The remaining planned '2.5 generation' He 219 was the E-1, which is described as having been derived from the He 219A-5. It was to have had a wooden tail assembly and wings and a forward-firing armament of two or four MK 108s mounted in a ventral fairing.

Alongside these 'paper' aeroplanes, mention should also be made of the He 219 V17, V19 and V33. In the order given, the V17 (He 219A-010/TL Wk-Nr 190060) was an engine testbed that was equipped with an underslung BMW 003 turbojet and DB 603G engines fitted with superchargers, while the V19 was used for cockpit pressurisation trials and was scheduled to be fitted with a three-man cockpit. This latter item was cancelled in late April 1944. Finally, the V33 (Wk-Nr 190063) was used by the radar manufacturer Telefunken for antenna trials – a programme that may have been intended to see the He 219 fitted with the dish aerial associated with the centimetric band FuG 240/1 *Berlin N1a* AI radar.

APPENDICES

COLOUR PLATES COMMENTARY

1
He 219 V1 Wk-Nr 219001 VG+LW, Rostock-Marienehe, early 1943
This profile shows the configuration of the He 219 V1 after modifications (smooth fuselage shape, lengthened engine nacelles and enlarged fins and rudders) that were undertaken by Heinkel during December 1942–January 1943. At this time, the aircraft was finished in *Farbton 22 schwarz* (black, RLM 22) overall, with *Farbton 21 weiß* (white, RLM 21) outline national markings. Its *Stammkenzeichen* (master identification code) was applied in *Farbton 77 dunkelgrau* (dark grey, RLM 77) on both sides of the aircraft's fuselage and beneath its wings. Wk-Nr 219001 was fitted with the He 219's early style of raised cockpit canopy, which was designed to allow for the installation of a rear-firing weapon.

2
He 219 V6 Wk-Nr 190006 DH+PV, Erprobungsstelle Rechlin, 1943
He 219 V6 was used for both trials with the FuG 202 AI intercept radar and as an ejector seat testbed (as shown here). For the latter, the rear section of the aircraft's cockpit canopy was discarded – a configuration that at one time also saw its FuG 202 dipoles removed. The V6 was the last He 219 prototype to feature the type's original stepped fuselage, small fins and rudders and short engine nacelles. Like the V1, Wk-Nr 190006 was finished in RLM 22 overall, with RLM 21 outline national markings and RLM 77 *Stammkenzeichen*. Note also the *V6* inscription in RLM 77 below the aircraft's windscreen.

3
He 219 V8 Wk-Nr 190008 DH+PX, Erprobungsstelle Rechlin, September 1943
This artwork shows the He 219 V8 as it was photographed at the Rechlin test centre on 3 September 1943. Wk-Nr 190008 almost certainly started life in an overall RLM 22 finish, which was subsequently oversprayed with a uniform coat of *Farbton 76 lichtblau/graublau* (light blue/grey blue, RLM 76). So adorned, the He 219 V8's national markings took the form of RLM 22 outlines, with its *Stammkenzeichen* being the same colour and presented on the sides of its fuselage and lower wing surfaces. Again, the He 219 V8 had the type's bulged style of cockpit canopy, featured an RLM 22 *V8* on the lower part of its fins and was fitted with four-bladed propellers.

4
He 219 V9 Wk-Nr 190009 G9+FB of *Stab*/I.NJG 1, Venlo, the Netherlands, June 1943
He 219 V9 is depicted here as it appeared when the aircraft made the type's first operational sortie on the night of 11–12 June 1943. Again, fitted with the He 219's early bulged style of cockpit canopy, Wk-Nr 190009 was finished in overall RLM 76 with RLM 22 outline national markings. Its *Verbandekenzeichen* was also presented in RLM 22, with the nightfighter's 'aircraft-in-*Staffel*' identification letter being in *Farbton 25 hellgrün* (bright green, RLM 25) and denoting its assignment to I./NJG 1's *Stab* flight. As was normal practice on operational He 219s, the G9 of Wk-Nr 190009's *Verbandekenzeichen* was applied in characters that were one-fifth the size of the FB lettering. Other features of note included the application of RLM 22 command chevrons on both sides of the aircraft's forward fuselage. On the night of 11–12 June 1943, G9+FB was flown into action by Major Werner Streib of *Stab* I./NJG 1.

5
He 219A G9+FK of 2./NJG 1, Venlo, the Netherlands, April 1944
When photographed on 18 April 1944, G9+FK was painted in the He 219's standard camouflage finish of RLM 76, with the uppersurfaces of its fuselage, wings and tailplanes being mottled in *Farbton 75 grauviolett* (violet grey, RLM 75). Elsewhere, the lower surfaces of G9+FK's starboard wing and the rear part of its starboard engine nacelle were finished in RLM 22 as a visual recognition feature. National markings took the form of solid RLM 22 swastikas, RLM 21/22 crosses beneath the aircraft's port wing and on its fuselage sides and RLM 21/22 outline crosses below its starboard wing and above both wings, respectively. Other points of interest are the *Englandblitz* badge on both sides of the aircraft's nose, the presentation of its 'aircraft-in-*Staffel*' letter (F) in 2./NJG 1's *Farbton 23 rot* (red, RLM 23) identification colour and the carriage of antenna arrays for both the FuG 212 and FuG 220 radar sets. On the occasion of this April 1944 flight, G9+FK was being flown by nightfighter ace Hauptmann Ernst-Wilhelm Modrow.

6
He 219A G9+SK of 2./NJG 1, Venlo, the Netherlands, summer 1944
Another 2./NJG 1 aircraft, G9+SK followed the He 219's standard RLM 75/76 camouflage scheme with what appears to have been an RLM 75 mottle over the type's normally plain RLM 76 fuselage sides. Another reading of this finish is that G9+SK had started life in an RLM 22/75/76 colour scheme, the RLM 22 elements of which had been subsequently oversprayed with RLM 76. Here, the fuselage mottling could have been areas of RLM 22 showing through the RLM 76 overspray. G9+SK's national markings are a mix of solid RLM 22 swastikas, RLM 21/22 fuselage crosses, a solid RLM 22 cross on the underside of the aircraft's port wing and outline RLM 22 crosses on its uppersurfaces. The propeller spinners were finished in RLM 22, with RLM 21 spirals, and its 'aircraft-in-*Staffel*' letter was applied in 2./NJG 1's RLM 23 identification colour.

7
He 219A-2 Wk-Nr 420331 G9+DB of *Stab* I./NJG 1, Venlo, the Netherlands, late summer 1944
This Schwechat-built He 219A-2 was finished in the type's standard RLM 75/76 camouflage scheme, with an application of RLM 22 on the underside of its starboard wing and engine nacelle. National markings (with the exception of an RLM 21 outline cross beneath the aircraft's RLM 22 wing) follow the He 219's standard pattern. Other points to note are the RLM 22 presentation of the aircraft's Wk-Nr on the outer faces of its fins and the use of the same colour for its *Verbandekenzeichen* (with the G9 in the usual one-fifth size). The underside RLM 22 colour is applied in a similar manner to that shown in profile five. Wk-Nr 420331 was amongst 45 He 219s found at Westerland following Germany's surrender.

8
He 219A G9+CH of 1./NJG 1, Münster-Handorf, Germany, late 1944
G9+CH may be another example of an RLM 22/75/76-finished He 219 whose undersides (apart from the lower sections of its port and, possibly, starboard engine nacelles) were subsequently oversprayed with RLM 76 in such a way as to create a mottled effect around its nose. The aircraft's national markings took

the form of solid RLM 22 swastikas, RLM 21/22 crosses on its fuselage sides and beneath its wings and RLM 22 outline crosses above its wings. Note also the RLM 21 outline to the nightfighter's RLM 22 'aircraft-in-*Staffel*' letter C, denoting its assignment to 1./NJG 1.

9
He 219A-2 Wk-Nr 290004 G9+DH of 1./NJG 1, Münster-Handorf, Germany, January 1945

This Schwechat-built He 219A-2 was another example of the practice of painting the underside of the aircraft's starboard wing and engine nacelle in RLM 22 as a visual recognition feature. Other points to note are the RLM 22 presentations of its Wk-Nr on the outer faces of the vertical fin; the washed out grey centres to its fuselage crosses; the style of its uppersurface RLM 75 mottle (probably created by overspraying a solid coat of RLM 75 with a tight network of RLM 76 lines); and the small RLM 22 *IV* beneath its windscreen, which denoted that it was fitted with a FuG 220 radar that operated on a spot frequency of 91 MHz. Again, it is possible that the aircraft's 'aircraft-in-*Staffel*' letter D was very thinly outlined in 1./NJG 1's RLM 21 *Staffel* colour. Wk-Nr 290004 suffered 40 per cent damage when its pilot, Unteroffizier Hugo Oppermann, hit an obstacle while undertaking an emergency landing at Paderborn on 1–2 February 1945.

10
He 219A G9+VL of 3./NJG 1, Münster-Handorf, Germany, February 1945

Like many other late-war Luftwaffe nightfighters, several He 219s had their uppersurface camouflage toned down with an overspray of *Farbton 81 dunkelbraun* (dark brown, RLM 81) and/or *Farbton 82 olivgrün* (olive green, RLM 82) to give the aircraft better ground concealment from marauding Allied fighter-bombers. G9+VL was one such aircraft, with other points of note including the RLM 22 finish on its lower starboard wing and engine nacelle; the solid RLM 21 or 77 presentation of the national marking beneath the same wing; and the *Farbton 27 gelb* (yellow, RLM 27) presentation of its 'aircraft-in-*Staffel*' letter denoting that it was assigned to NJG 1's 3rd *Staffel*. Again, the one-fifth size RLM 22 application of its *Geschwader* code (G9) is barely discernible against the RLM 81/82 mottle that has been applied to the aircraft's fuselage sides.

11
He 219A 1L+M? of NJGr 10, Finow, Germany, early 1945

1L+M? is another example of an He 219A whose uppersurfaces and sides were given a ground concealment camouflage of RLM 81/82 squiggles over their original RLM 75/76 finish. Other points of interest are the greying out of the centres of the aircraft's RLM 21/22 fuselage crosses; the painting out (with RLM 21?) of its 'aircraft-in-*Staffel*' and *Staffel* identification letters on the starboard side of its fuselage; the RLM 21 propeller spinners with a single RLM 22 spiral; and what may be an area of RLM 22 paint beneath its starboard engine nacelle – it is not known whether such an application was made to port. One-fifth-size RLM 22 presentations of NJGr 10's identifier code 1L appear on both sides of the aircraft's fuselage, accompanied by an RLM 22 'aircraft-in-*Staffel*' letter M to port. It has been suggested that this aircraft belonged to tactics and training unit 2./NJGr 10, which would had made its *Staffel* identifier the letter K.

12
He 219A-2 Wk-Nr 290068, Rostock-Marienehe, Germany, autumn 1944

A number of Rostock-Marienehe-produced He 219As within the 290054 to 290078 and 290111 to 290129 Wk-Nr blocks are reported to have been delivered in the factory-applied RLM 22/75/76 camouflage scheme seen here, with RLM 22 covering the aircrafts' undersurfaces, fuselage sides and vertical fins and rudders. Wk-Nr 290068 exemplifies this scheme, and also features RLM 21 outline swastikas and fuselage and underwing crosses teamed, it is assumed, with RLM 22 outline crosses on the wing uppersurfaces. Other points of note are the RLM 21 presentation of the aircraft's Wk-Nr on the outer faces of its fins, the solid RLM 76 finish applied to the fronts of its engine nacelles (a feature seen on most He 219As regardless of their overall camouflage) and the RLM 21 spiral added to its RLM 22 propeller spinners.

13
He 219A-2 Wk-Nr 290123 G9+TH of 1./NJG 1, Westerland, Germany, April 1945

Like Wk-Nr 290068 seen in the previous profile, G9+TH was finished in the factory-applied RLM 22/75/76 camouflage scheme. Other points to note include the patchy RLM 21 or 77 presentation of the aircraft's Wk-Nr on the outer surfaces of its fins; the presentation of its one-fifth size *Geschwader* identifier (G9) and its full size *Staffel* identifier (H) in RLM 77; the presentation of its 'aircraft-in-*Staffel*' letter *T* in the form of a white outline (signifying ownership by 1./NJG 1); and the *V1* frequency code in RLM 22 beneath the windscreen, signifying that the nightfighter was fitted with a FuG 220 radar that operated on a spot frequency of 73 MHz. Elsewhere, the 'aircraft-in-*Staffel*' letter has been applied over a previous, painted-out identifier, and there are areas of RLM 76 showing through the RLM 22 on the He 219's rear fuselage and port fin. This may be suggestive that the RLM 22 application was made over an original RLM 76 finish. Wk-Nr 290123 was also amongst the 45 He 219s found at Westerland at war's end.

14
He 219A-010/TL (He 219 V17) Wk-Nr 190060 PK+QJ, Hörsching/Linz, Austria, May 1945

When delivered in September 1943, this Schwechat-built aircraft was fitted with a belly-mounted BMW 003 turbojet to boost its dash speed. The nightfighter was given the designation He 219A-010/TL, also known as the He 219 V17, as a result of this modification. In November 1944, the aircraft's auxiliary jet engine was removed and it was converted into the 'special testing' platform depicted here. At war's end, Wk-Nr 190060 was captured at Hörsching/Linz airfield in Austria. Points to note are the greyed-out centres to its fuselage crosses, the 'cancellation' (in RLM 77?) of the V17 designator on its starboard fin, the apparent RLM 22 finish of the undersides of the engine nacelles and the presentation of its *Stammkenzeichen* on both sides of the fuselage and beneath the wings.

15
He 219A-065 Wk-Nr 190179 of 2./NJG 1, Westerland, Germany, May 1945

Wk-Nr 190179 represents one of several anonymous He 219s that were found abandoned post-May 1945. Points of interest are the greyed-out centres of its fuselage crosses, the solid RLM 75 starboard fin, the abbreviated presentation of its Wk-Nr (179) on the outer face of the same fin and an apparent area of RLM 76 overspray where the nightfighter's fuselage *Verbandekenzeichen* would normally have been carried. This aircraft served with 2./NJG 1 from May 1944 through to war's end.

16
He 219A-7 Wk-Nr 310193 (unit and location unknown)

Wk-Nr 310193 is another example of an anonymous late-war He 219A. Points of interest about this Rostock-Marienehe-built aircraft include the tail warning radar antenna projecting aft from the rear of the nightfighter, the greyed-out centres of its fuselage crosses, the heavy exhaust staining on the undersides of its engine nacelles and the nature of its uppersurface RLM 75/76 camouflage.

17
He 219A-7 Wk-Nr 310189 D5+CL formerly of 3./NJG 3, RAE Farnborough, Hampshire, autumn 1945

D5+CL, one of 25 He 219s captured by the British at Grove in May 1945, was allocated the AM number 22 prior to being displayed in an exhibition of captured German aircraft that was held at Farnborough during October–November 1945. Points to note are the obscuring of the aircraft's *Verbandekenzeichen* with one of the RAF's grey camouflage paints; the application of RAF roundels and fin flashes; the *Vl* designator (signifying installation of a FuG 220 radar operating on a spot frequency of 73 MHz) beneath the windscreen; the faint RLM 21 spirals around the RLM 76 propeller spinners; the possible installation of a FuG 220 tail warning antenna; and what appears to be RLM 22 paint application on the undersides of the engine nacelles.

18
He 219A-2 Wk-Nr 290126 D5+BL formerly of 3./NJG 3, RAE Farnborough, Hampshire, autumn 1945

Like Wk-Nr 310189, D5+BL was captured by the British at Grove in May 1945. The aircraft was allocated the AM number 20 when it was subsequently brought to Britain for evaluation. Points to note include the RLM 21 spirals round the nightfighter's RLM 22 propeller spinners, its overall RLM 22/75/76 camouflage scheme, the overpainting of its original national markings and *Verbandekenzeichen*, the application of RAF roundels and fin flashes and the RLM 21 presentation of its Wk-Nr on the outer faces of the fins. RLM 21/23 warning stripes were also applied to this aircraft's lower FuG 220 radar antennas and ventral FuG 16 radio aerial – markings seen on a number of He 219s.

19
He 219A-2 Wk-Nr 290060, Cherbourg, France, July 1945

Captured by the British in May 1945, this Rostock-Marienehe-built aircraft was one of three He 219s handed over to the USAAF in June 1945 and shipped to the United States for evaluation. Points of interest include the application of American 'stars and bars', the removal of the aircraft's FuG 220 radar antenna, the *Vl* designator beneath its windscreen, the apparent areas of RLM 22 paint on the undersides of the engine nacelles and the *U.S.A. 9* inscription applied in black to the rear of the aircraft's fuselage. This is not the He 219 currently on display at the Smithsonian's Steven F. Udvar-Hazy Center in Virginia, although that example (Wk-Nr 290202) does feature Wk-Nr 290060's fins and rudders.

20
He 219A-7 Wk-Nr 310106, RAF Night Fighter Development Wing, RAF Ford, West Sussex, June 1945

Without doubt, Wk-Nr 310106 was the most interesting He 219 brought to Britain for evaluation at the end of the war in Europe. To the best of the author's knowledge, it was the only He 219 to have been photographed equipped with both the 162–187 MHz band FuG 218 AI radar and the FuG 350 centimetric radar homing device. Points of interest include the *Vl* code beneath the aircraft's windscreen (indicating that it had been equipped with 73 MHz spot frequency FuG 220 radar, and that it was retrofitted with FuG 218); the FuG 350 antenna blister above its cockpit canopy; the installation of the distinctive FuG 218 antenna array; the apparent RLM 22 finish of the underside of its engine nacelles; the application of RAF roundels and fin flashes; the painting out of its original *Verbandekenzeichen* (which appears to have included the letters EH, suggesting an assignment to 1./NJG 1); and the RLM 21 spirals round its RLM 22 propeller spinners. Again, it has been reported, but not confirmed, that its fuselage roundels were in fact of the French red/white/blue type rather than the British blue/white/red configuration shown here.

BIBLIOGRAPHY

Documents

D (Luft) T.2219 A-0 *Flugzeug-Handbuch Teil 8A – He 219 A-0 Schußwaffenlage* (February 1944)
L.Dv.T.2219 (N)/We *He 219 (N) Schußwaffenlage* (October 1943)
L.Dv.T.2219 A-0/Fl *He 219 A-0 Bedenungsvorschrift-Fl* (March 1944)

Books

Boiten, Theo, *Nachtjagd Combat Archive 1943 (Parts 2 and 3), 1944 (Parts 1 to 5) and 1945* (Red Kite, 2018–22)
Butler, Phil, *War Prizes – An Illustrated Survey of German, Italian and Japanese Aircraft Brought to Allied Countries During and After the Second World War* (Midland Counties, 1994)
Ferguson, R Francis, *Heinkel He 219 – An Illustrated History of the Third Reich's Dedicated Home-Defence Nightfighter* (Air Research, 2020)
Franks, Richard A, *The Heinkel He 219 Uhu – A Detailed Guide to the Luftwaffe's Ultimate Nightfighter* (Valiant Wings Publishing, 2021)
Remp, Roland, *Heinkel He 219 – An Illustrated History of Germany's Premier Nightfighter* (Schiffer Publishing, 2000)

INDEX

Note: page numbers in **bold** refer to illustrations, plates and captions

aircraft
    Arado Ar 234: **77**
    Ju 188: 11–12, 13–14, 15–16
    Lancaster 22
    Mosquito 21, **30**, 54, **58**, 76–77
    see also Heinkel He 219
airframe **73**, 78, 80–81
armament
    20mm MG 151/20 cannon 9, 34, 35, 77, 85, 90, 91
    30mm MK 108 cannon 14, 34, 77, 85, 86, **89**, 90, 91
    37mm BK 3.7 cannon 31
    layout and housing **15**, **87**, **88**, **89**
    machine guns 34, 91
    Schräge Musik installation 14, 34, 64, 77, 85, 86, **89**, 90, 91
armour **12**, **13**, 33

Baake, Oberleutnant Werner 25–28, 30, 32, 46–47, 49–53, 55–59, **55**, 61, 63, 66–67, 69
Bettaque, Feldwebel 28, 30, 49, 52, 57, 59, 63, 66–67, 69–70
Böhmer, Feldwebel Ernst **2–3**
Braham, Wg Cdr J R D 'Bob' 20, **21**
Brown, Capt Eric 'Winkle' 75, 76, **77**

cockpits and canopies cp.**3–4** (37, 92), 80, **80**, 81, **81**, **83**, **84**, 87

ejector seats 16, 77, 79, 81–83, **82**, **83**
engines
    BMW 003: 52, 91
    DB 603: 8, 9, 14, 16, 78, 86, 87, 88, **90**, 91
    Jumo 213: 16, 66, 78, 88
    Jumo 222: 90, 91, **91**
    tests 23–24

Fischer, Feldwebel Helmut 12–13, **18**, 59, 66–67
Förster, Major Paul **2–3**, 26, 32, 46, 49, 53
Frank, Hauptmann Hans-Dieter 18, 19, 20, 22
Frankenhauser, Unteroffizier Franz 50, 54, 57
Freydag, Dr 15–16
Fries, Leutnant Otto-Heinrich 31–32, **32**, 48–49, 56–57, 61–62, 66–67

Galland, Oberst Adolf 14
Göring, Reichsmarschall Hermann 15
Gotter, Feldwebel Erich 18, 20
Gregory, Flt Lt Bill **21**

Habricht, Feldwebel Fritz 'Pitt' 20, 31, 35, 63
Hager, Oberleutnant Johannes 31, 46
Heinkel, Professor Ernst 8, 9–10
Heinkel He 219
    captured by Allies 71–75
    interiors **74**, **75**, 79, 81, **81**, **84**
    name 15, 79
    problems and performance 34, 56, 75–79
Heinkel He 219 models
    He 219 V1: **6**, 8–11, **10**, **11**
    He 219 V1 Wk-Nr 219001 VG+LW 17, cp.**1** (36, 92)
    He 219 V2: 10–11, 13
    He 219 V6 Wk-Nr 190006 DH+PV cp.**2** (36, 92), 82, **83**
    He 219 V7: 11, 12, 21
    He 219 V8: 11
    He 219 V8 Wk-Nr 190008 DH+PX **17**, cp.**3** (37, 92)
    He 219 V9: 11, 12
    He 219 V9 Wk-Nr 190009 G9+FB 12–13, 18, **18**, **19**, cp.**4** (37, 92)
    He 219 V10 G9+DB 19, 20
    He 219 V12: 19, 20, 26
    He 219A G9+CH cp.**8** (39, 93), 56, 57, 65, 69
    He 219A G9+FK **28**, **29**, cp.**5** (38, 92)
    He 219A G9+SK cp.**6** (38, 92)
    He 219A G9+VL cp.**10** (40, 93)
    He 219A 1L+M? cp.**11** (41, 93)
    He 219A-0: 77–78, 85–86, **87**, **88**
    He 219A-0 Wk-Nr 190188: **2–3**, 31, 34
    He 219A-0 Wk-Nr 210903: 29, 71, 73, **73**
    He 219A-042 Wk-Nr 190113 DV+DI 82, **82**
    He 219A-2: 16–17, 86–87
    He 219A-2 Wk-Nr 290004 G9+DH cp.**9** (40, 93), **60**, 63
    He 219A-2 Wk-Nr 290013: **25**
    He 219A-2 Wk-Nr 290060 cp.**19** (45, 94), 71, 73, 74
    He 219A-2 Wk-Nr 290068 cp.**12** (41, 93), **52**
    He 219A-2 Wk-Nr 290123 G9+TH cp.**13** (42, 93), **51**, 71
    He 219A-2 Wk-Nr 290126 D5+BL cp.**18** (44, 94), **71**, 71
    He 219A-2 Wk-Nr 290202: 71, 73–74, **74**, **75**, 81
    He 219A-2 Wk-Nr 420331 G9+DB cp.**7** (39, 92), 71
    He 219A-7: 17, 87
    He 219A-7 Wk-Nr 310106: 17, cp.**20** (45, 94), **68**, 69, 71–72
    He 219A-7 Wk-Nr 310109: 59, 71, 72
    He 219A-7 Wk-Nr 310189 D5+CL cp.**17** (44, 94), **62**, 71, 72, **72**
    He 219A-7 Wk-Nr 310193 cp.**16** (43, 94)
    He 219A-010/TL (He 219 V17) Wk-Nr 190060 PK+QJ 14, cp.**14** (42, 93), 91
    He 219A-065 Wk-Nr 190179: 31, cp.**15** (43, 94)
    He 219D-1: 17, 88
    paper designs 88–91
Henseler, Oberleutnant Wilhelm 29, 32, 51, 61, 66
Herter, Unteroffizier 27–28, 82
Hittler, Leutnant Werner 34, 35, 47, 50
Hüschens, Hauptmann Werner 50, 54

Irving, Flg Off G S 54

Kammhuber, *General der Flieger* Josef **8**, 9, 12, 14, 18
Karlewski, Major Hans 28, 32, 48, 49
Keune, Unteroffizier Hans 48, 61

Luftwaffe: NJG 1: 15, 19, 20, 22, 33, 47
    I./NJG 1: **2–3**, 10–11, 12–13, 18–23, 25–67, 78
    1./NJG 1: 29, 46, 50, **60**, 61, 63, 65, 68, 69–71
    II./NJG 1: 29, 30–32, 33, 46, 47, 48
    2./NJG 1: **19**, 25, 28, 29, 31, 46, 51, 55, 57, 61
    3./NJG 1: 20, 26, 27, 31, 34, 55, 59, 62, 66–67, 68
    5./NJG 1: 52
    6./NJG 1: 47
    8./NJG 1: 67
Luftwaffe: NJG 3: **62**, 68
    I./NJG 3: 60, 61, 66
    II./NJG 3: 47
    III./NJG 3: 61
    IV./NJG 3: 47
    4./NJG 3: 50
Luftwaffe NJG 5: 69
Luftwaffe: NJGr 10: 27, **27**, 48, 50
    2./NJGr 10: 33, 47, 48, 50, 51, 53, 55
Luftwaffe: NJSt *Finnland/Norwegen* 49–50, 51, 53, 54, 55, 60, 62

Mauss, Leutnant Ernst 35, 62
Mellows, Flt Lt Paul 59
Meurer, Hauptmann Manfred 19, 20, 21, 22, **24**, 26
Milch, Generaloberst Erhard 7–8, **7**, 9–10, 11, 13–14
Miller, Wilfrid 50
Millington, Flg Off G 54
Modrow, Hauptmann Ernst-Wilhelm 15, 21, 23, **23**, 25–33, 35, 47, 50–51, 53, 56, 61, 63, 65, 67, 69–70
Morlock, Feldwebel Wilhelm 32–33, 46, 47, 49, 53, 55

Nabrich, Oberleutnant Josef 26, 31–32, 35, 46–47, 50, 52, 55–56
Neff, Unteroffizier 63–64, 67, 69

Oloff, Oberleutnant Heinz 59, 66, 67
Oppermann, Unteroffizier Hugo 46, 63

paintwork and markings **11**, **17**, **20**, **25**, **27**, cp.**1–20** (36–45, 92–94), **51**, **52**
Peltz, Generalmajor Dietrich 12, 75–76, **76**
Perbix, Gefreiter Werner 27–28, 82
Prietze, Leutnant Jürgen 55, 56, 58

radar
    FuG202: 8, **17**, cp.**2** (36, 92), 78, 83, 84
    FuG212/220: 13, 19, 20, 23, 27, **29**, 35, cp.**5** (38, 92), cp.**13** (42, 93), 49, **52**, 60, 65, 70, 72, 73, 78, **81**, 83, 84–85, **85**, **86**
    FuG218 cp.**20** (45, 94), **68**, 69, 71–72, 76, 78, 83, 84
    homing devices 35, cp.**20** (45, 94), 50, 53, 62–63, **68**, 71, 72, 78, 83
    reliability 78
radios 8, 23–24, 53, **60**, 83, 86
Rauer, Feldwebel Alfred 27, 30–31, 32, 33
Reeves, Flt Lt Nevil 28
Richer, Oberfeldwebel Johannes 48, **48**
Rosséguier de Miremont, Hauptmann Alexander Graf 63, 70–71

Schäfer-Suren, Major Gert 46, 49
Scheibe, Oberfeldwebel Gerhard 22, 26
Schmidt, Generalmajor Joseph 'Beppo' 15
Schneider, Gefreiter Erich 21, 23, 25–31, 49, 61, 69–70
Schoenert, Major Rudolf 15, 27, 48, **48**
Shön, Leutnant Walter 20, 22
Sieben, Feldwebel Hans 59, 62, 64–65, 67
Staffa, Feldwebel 48, 57, 62, 63, 66, 67, 83
Streib, Major Werner 10, 11, 12–13, 14, 18, **18**, **19**, 68
Ströhlein, Feldwebel Josef 29, 48, 61
Strüning, Oberleutnant Heinz 20, 31, 32, 34, 35, 46–47, 48–49

Thurner, Oberleutnant Ruppert 55, 66–67
Thurow, Feldwebel Günther 63–64, 67, 69

Udet, Generaloberst Ernst 7–8
undercarriages 34, 78, 80, **87**

Weber, Feldwebel Heinz 27, 30–31, 32
windscreen shields **12**, **33**, 34
Wollenhaupt, Unteroffizier Werner 54, 55, 57